ASIAN POLITICAL, ECONOMIC AND SECURITY ISSUES

THE THIRD SINO-JAPANESE WAR

DREAM OF PACIFIC EMPIRE

ASIAN POLITICAL, ECONOMIC AND SECURITY ISSUES

Additional books in this series can be found on Nova's website
under the Series tab.

Additional E-books in this series can be found on Nova's website
under the E-books tab.

THE THIRD SINO-JAPANESE WAR

DREAM OF PACIFIC EMPIRE

Guang Wu

Nova Science Publishers, Inc.
New York

Copyright ©2012 by Nova Science Publishers, Inc.

For permission to use material from this book please contact us:
Telephone 631-231-7269; Fax 631-231-8175
Web Site: http://www.novapublishers.com

NOTICE TO THE READER

The Publisher has taken reasonable care in the preparation of this book, but makes no expressed or implied warranty of any kind and assumes no responsibility for any errors or omissions. No liability is assumed for incidental or consequential damages in connection with or arising out of information contained in this book. The Publisher shall not be liable for any special, consequential, or exemplary damages resulting, in whole or in part, from the readers' use of, or reliance upon, this material. Any parts of this book based on government reports are so indicated and copyright is claimed for those parts to the extent applicable to compilations of such works.

Independent verification should be sought for any data, advice or recommendations contained in this book. In addition, no responsibility is assumed by the publisher for any injury and/or damage to persons or property arising from any methods, products, instructions, ideas or otherwise contained in this publication.

This publication is designed to provide accurate and authoritative information with regard to the subject matter covered herein. It is sold with the clear understanding that the Publisher is not engaged in rendering legal or any other professional services. If legal or any other expert assistance is required, the services of a competent person should be sought. FROM A DECLARATION OF PARTICIPANTS JOINTLY ADOPTED BY A COMMITTEE OF THE AMERICAN BAR ASSOCIATION AND A COMMITTEE OF PUBLISHERS.

Additional color graphics may be available in the e-book version of this book.

Library of Congress Cataloging-in-Publication Data

Wu, Guang, 1962-
 The third Sino-Japanese war : dream of Pacific Empire / author, Guang Wu.
  p. cm.
 Includes bibliographical references and index.
 Summary: "China was defeated during the first Sino-Japanese war and Japan was defeated during World War II including the second Sino-Japanese war. Since then, the relationship between China and Japan has varied between good and bad. This book does not discuss various trivial disputes between China and Japan; instead it considers the real cause, which is the competition to become a Pacific Empire, which would lead to the third Sino-Japanese war and would eventually challenge the current Pacific Empire, the United States of America. Under such a circumstance, the book discusses various aspects on the third Sino-Japanese war from a Chinese viewpoint."--Publisher's description.
 ISBN 978-1-61324-489-0 (softcover : alk. paper) 1. China--Foreign relations--Japan. 2. Japan--Foreign relations--China. 3. China--Foreign economic relations--Japan. 4. Japan--Foreign economic relations--China. 5. China--Military policy. 6. Japan--Military policy. 7. National security--China. 8. National security--Japan. I. Title.
 DS740.5.J3W7817 2011
 327.51052--dc22
                          2011013415

Published by Nova Science Publishers, Inc. † New York

DEDICATED TO MY BELOVED PARENTS
QINGHE WU AND HEQING ZHOU

CONTENTS

PREFACE

Impossible is a word to be found only in the dictionary of fools.
— Napoleon Bonaparte

As a researcher myself, I sometimes feel that we, scientist, find nothing impossible at least in our imaginations. When I turn my attention to politicians, I find that politicians feel everything possible at least in their imaginations. I am not sure whether philosophers hold a similar view, i.e. everything is possible or nothing is impossible.

If everything is possible, then the third Sino-Japanese war would be possible. If the third Sino-Japanese war is possible, we should elaborate it from different views and angles in order to make the third Sino-Japanese war impossible.

On the other hand, if everything is possible, why we cannot make the non-occurrence of the third Sino-Japanese war possible?

How can we make the third Sino-Japanese war impossible? This was the question I attempted to answer before writing this book, i.e. the initial aim was to answer a question. In the Essays of Francis Bacon [1], there are such words: "Question was asked of Demosthenes, what was the chief part of an orator? He answered, action; what next? Action; what next again? Action."

Perhaps, we need to ask what the chief part of action is? My answer would be options. Without options, we cannot take action. Then we need to ask what the chief part of an option is? My answer would be analysis. Without analysis, we cannot have options. Therefore, the aim of this book changed from answering a question to analyzing in order to get options.

Guang Wu
February 21, 2011
China

Chapter 1

PACIFIC EMPIRE

His Majesty the Kaiser said Germany's future lies on the sea.
— Stephen King-Hall, Diary of a U-boat Commander [2]

As the world entered the 21st century, we can easily find that three world economic giants, US, Japan and China, are all located around the Pacific Ocean. This phenomenon is very similar to what we have seen in the 19th and 20th centuries, when the world economic giants were exclusively located along the North Atlantic Ocean. Of course, the large-scale wars, where both parties had equal or similar powers, occurred in surrounding countries along the Atlantic coasts.

Since World War II, NATO has become the queen of the Atlantic Ocean, while the US has become both an Atlantic and Pacific Empire. NATO is in fact composed of countries from both sides of Atlantic Ocean, and the NATO military power from both sides of Atlantic Ocean can easily dominate the Atlantic Ocean.

It is mostly likely that the great politicians and statesmen, who lived in the 20th century, did not anticipate that the next world focus would be the Pacific Ocean, actually the North Pacific Ocean. Therefore we have not yet seen the creation of the North Pacific Treaty Organization. Arguably, the US is only a partial Pacific Empire, because there is no strong military organization on the western Pacific Ocean to support the US's domination. This fact that the US is a half Pacific Empire is mainly due to the disarming of Japan after World War II.

Under such a circumstance, the world powers have to reorganize their focus switching from the Atlantic Ocean to the Pacific Ocean. Certainly the Pacific Ocean has replaced the Atlantic Ocean to become the focus of the 21st century.

The question is, which country will dominate the western Pacific Ocean? Currently, China and Japan are frontrunners pursuing the domination of western

Pacific Ocean, hence the current disputes and disagreements between China and Japan, on various trivial issues, are all pretexts although many people have yet to think so.

1.1 EMPIRE OF SEA

Historically, the empire, which plays an important role in human civilization, and political role in regional and global affairs, is the empire built along the seacoast. For example, the Athens Empire and the Roman Empire were built around Mediterranean Sea, the Russian Empire was built along the Baltic Sea after defeating Swedish power, the Spanish Empire dominated the Atlantic Ocean, and the British Empire dominated the world sea, mainly the Atlantic Ocean. It is, in fact, only the American Empire that dominates the world sea, mainly the Atlantic and Pacific Oceans.

Many historical figures, whose nations were confined far away from the sea, realized that the future of their nations would be closely related to the sea, and switched their national policy focus from inland to the sea. An example of such a historical figure was Peter the Great of Russia.

In this context, the Chinese Empire, although it existed for several thousands of years, was an empire of land. It is quite strange and very pitiful that China has fairly long seacoasts, which are totally different from the frozen seacoasts in Russia, but did not develop a sea empire. Sadly, the sea surrounding China confines the Chinese civilization and culture, which cannot spread beyond the Chinese territory. So, we could say that Chinese Empire was an inland empire. Consequently, we would arguably say that the Chinese Empire was a local empire with little, if any, influence on world civilization and development. Although many Chinese scholars claimed that the ancient Chinese GDP accounted for a large portion of world GDP, this by no means contributed to the world simply because China was not a sea empire, which could use her resources to influence the world. The Chinese emperors never dreamt to extend their border beyond the sea, perhaps due to the fact that many Chinese emperors came from inland of China and they were seasick.

Since the end of World War II, the UK's economy and military power was reduced dramatically in comparison with other world powers and potential world powers, but the UK is still playing a key role in international affairs, and her influence goes far beyond her economic reach, being not proportional to her economic strength. This is so arguably because the UK once dominated the world sea.

Let's look at several other countries, which had the geographical chance to become a sea empire but failed to do so.

Arguably, ancient Egypt had a situation somewhat similar to China. The geographical location of ancient Egypt was relatively similar to China: the threats to ancient Egypt could not come from south because of the deserts, while the threats to ancient China could not come from south because of the sea. With the open Mediterranean Sea, as well as the size of Egyptian population, ancient Egypt could arguably have had a great potential to dominate the Mediterranean Sea. However, this was not the case for the ancient Egypt. Similarly, ancient China had several open seas and the Great Wall to defend the threats from north, this would have given China a geographic chance to dominate the western Pacific Ocean. However, this was not the case. Actually, the sea and the desert helped Egypt to develop her great civilization, and the sea and the Great Wall helped China to develop her great civilization independent from other civilizations.

Another puzzling case would be Indonesia, whose geographic advantage could have provided a real opportunity for Indonesia to find and colonize Australia, and then to dominate South Pacific Ocean. However, this was not the case.

Similarly, we can ask why India did not dominate the Indian Ocean to become a dominant power for South Asia and East Africa, then to colonize East Africa and so on.

1.2 LAST OCEAN WITHOUT QUEEN

In modern history, Japan attempted twice to dominate at least the western part of the Pacific Rim and the western Pacific Ocean if not the whole Pacific Ocean. For this reason, the Japanese invoked three wars along the western Pacific Ocean: the first Sino-Japanese war (1894-1895), the Russo-Japanese war (1904-1905), and the second Sino-Japanese war (1937-1945) followed by World War II.

Therefore, the historical message is very clear: any country with the ambition to become an empire, a regional power or a world power in modern terms, should dominate the sea. In this regard, the former Soviet Union, whose focus was misplaced on Central Europe, did not attempt to become a Pacific Empire. This might be a possible reason for losing the competition with the American Empire that dominates both the Atlantic and Pacific Oceans. Unfortunately, the current Russia still has little focus on Pacific Ocean, thus she is a second rate nation in world affairs.

Over last 30 years, China is rapidly transforming from a closed inland country into an open country although China is still not a sea-oriented country. However, it is natural that China would have big and bigger ambitions with her increased economic power.

The question is whether China will become a sea-oriented country overcoming her previous tradition. If the answer to this question is yes, then we expect endless conflicts, disputes and disagreements between China and Japan.

Actually, Japan dominates the western Pacific Ocean before China emerged on the world stage. At the end of Japanese film, Battle of the Japan Sea [3], a Japanese policymaker asked another policymaker if Japan would wage a war against the US, and the other policymaker answered: Yes and we must prepare it for it now. This is very suggestive because it means that any country along the Pacific coast could prepare a war in order to dominate the Pacific Ocean and become a Pacific Empire. If so, then we would expect to see a war between China and Japan, which would be the third Sino-Japanese war. No matter what the results of the third Sino-Japanese war would be, the winning country, either China or Japan, would certainly challenge the current Atlantic and Pacific Empire, the United States of America.

On the other hand, if the Russian Empire and the Soviet Union would have had the ambition to become a Pacific Empire, then we would have seen the people's migration from the European part of Russia and the Soviet Union to the Pacific Rim just as American history showed the migration of Americans from the east to west coasts [4]. Perhaps the Russo-Japanese war made Russia give up the ambition to become a Pacific Empire.

Latin America has the potential to become the Atlantic and Pacific Empire, not only because Latin America has geographic advantages similar to the US, which is located between the Atlantic and Pacific Oceans, but also because economic development in Latin America is fast progressing. Latin America has the chance to dominate the southern Atlantic and Pacific Oceans.

It is hard to say whether the Chinese people comprehend the concept of a Pacific Empire. This is so because (i) the Chinese educational system describes an empire with a negative tone, and in principle the Chinese people and the government deny imperialism; (ii) more importantly the Chinese people have yet to realize that the essential cause for current conflicts and disputes between China and Japan and between China and the US is the question of domination of Pacific Ocean. Thus, domination of Pacific Ocean is the real cause underlying the current relationship between China and Japan and between China and the US.

1.3 WAYS TOWARDS PACIFIC EMPIRE

If the Pacific Ocean is the last ocean without a queen, then which country has the potential to dominate the Pacific Ocean? The answer to this question seems very clear: the US, Russia, Japan and China are the countries with the potential to become the Queen of the Pacific Ocean, and establish a Pacific Empire in the 21st century.

Let us look at what the aim is to become the Pacific Empire. In human history, we can see that various previous Empires used their superiority on the sea to gain benefits in trades with remote countries, to obtain gold, silver, jewelry and other resources from less developed countries, to colonize less developed countries, to enslave other nations, and so on. Of course, these great ancient Empires did not include local and inland empires such as the Chinese Empires. In this view, arguably the sea empires exploited foreign countries in order to benefit themselves while the inland empires exploited their own countrymen in order to benefit a small group of powerful people living inside inland empires.

It is certain that sea empires got all the benefits from underdeveloped nations, which could be the reason why so many people and countries hate imperialism, and the reason why sea empires need strong military power.

Although international communities have made great efforts for decades, even a century, it appears that the current international orders and justice still cannot offer what a sea empire wants. Perhaps this is the reason why the US, Russia, Japan and China are yearning to become a Pacific Empire.

At this moment, we, the ordinary people in the world, should ask whether we have exhausted our ways to create a better mechanism to let each country be fairly treated rather than pursuing the position of Pacific Empire?

In this western Pacific part of world,three potential countries, Japan, China and Russia, are simultaneously getting on track to become the Pacific Empire. Human history shows that the only way to accomplish this is war. We, the people living in this part of the Pacific Rim should definitely say that we do not need the war!

Still, we should ask the US, Japan, Russia and China whether becoming the Pacific Empire is the only way towards becoming the world power in the 21st century.

In some sense, both China and Japan hope to become a world power in the 21st century. Unfortunately, both the Chinese people and the Japanese people cannot create a systematic theory related to the distribution of social wealth and excusion of social justice to become a world power [5]. Accordingly, the only imaginable way left for both China and Japan to become a real world power would be war, through which either China or Japan can dominate the western Pacific Ocean and eventually become a Pacific Empire.

This is to say, with both China and Japan trending towards world power, the historical trend is to use military power. However, it is very hard to define the aim for a potential third Sino-Japanese war. If one cannot define a clear aim for this war, it would be difficult to initiate a full-scale war without a clear definition. Thus, we, the Chinese people, should ask ourselves what China would like to achieve through the third Sino-Japanese war? Meanwhile the Japanese people should ask themselves what Japan would like to achieve through the third Sino-Japanese war?

Perhaps, we should ask ourselves another question before answering the abovementioned question, that is, is there any conflicting area between China and Japan? Are China and Japan trying to colonize a same country? Does a trading war occur between China and Japan? Does China organize an alliance to undermine Japanese interests? Does Japan organize an alliance to undermine Chinese interests? Do Chinese and Japanese interests collide heavily in somewhere in the world? Is the war the way to become a regional or world power?

During the first Sino-Japanese war, the Japanese interest in China seemed to have little conflict with the interests from European powers; otherwise the European powers would have done something to help China. During the second Sino-Japanese war, Japanese interest in China had significant conflicts with the interests from the US, and to lesser degree with European powers. From this viewpoint, the US and European governments supported and helped China during the second Sino-Japanese war.

Currently, the time prior to the third Sino-Japanese war, we could see that the Japanese interest has very few conflicts with the interests from the US and other European countries inside China. This is a different situation from the second Sino-Japanese war. On the other hand, China had almost no conflicts with Japan, European powers and the US beyond the Chinese borders during the first and second Sino-Japanese wars.

But now China seems to have many conflicts in interests with Japan, European countries and the US beyond the Chinese borders. We could suggest that there would be few conflicts between China and Japan when both economies are complementary, i.e. Japan produces high quality and high-tech products while China produces low quality and low-tech products. However this assumption does not seem to be the case.

Chapter 2

WHO NEEDS THE THIRD SINO-JAPANESE WAR?

At any rate, whether it was the original plan or not, such was the result.
— Jacob Abbott, Richard I [6]

The war is the focus of all the countries of interests, which can come from regional powers, world powers, internal powers, political power, economic power, religious influence, media influence, ideological difference, and various ambitions. As the concentration of solar rays can make a fire, the concentration of various interests and ambitions would make a war because it is only in the form of war that various interests and ambitions can be settled and trivial disputes can be solved. Similarly, the third Sino-Japanese war would be the last solution to seal the hatred in many people's mind, and accomplish the ambition of being the Pacific Empire in many Chinese and Japanese people's dreams. Of course the new hatred will be planted during the third Sino-Japanese war, which will be settled in the far future.

It would be either China or Japan or both China and Japan themselves, who have the intention to initiate the third Sino-Japanese war. The international communities do not favor this war, so the chance of occurrence of war would be small. Because the international communities would be strongly against this war, this would lead to the miscarriage of the third Sino-Japanese war at a very earlier stage.

Therefore, the conflict between China and Japan is not a regional issue, but is the focus of many interests and ambitions. If our logic goes along this way, then we should look at who needs the third Sino-Japanese war, who has money to support the third Sino-Japanese war, and the possible way to promote the third Sino-Japanese war?

The current atmosphere at the international level slightly favors the conflicts and frictions. This is so because we have not yet seen that any international organization, such as the UN, or that any international media have the intention to reduce the tension between China and Japan. Currently we are not sure whether China's policy that China does not allow intervention from other countries into Chinese affairs contributes to the present atmosphere.

The convergence of various groups of interests is likely to direct China, i.e. the international forces would promote the possibility of a third Sino-Japanese war, because this war would likely defeat China although currently many Chinese people do not think so.

On the other hand, fortunately, we also have not yet seen envoys from various blocs gather together to plan to form new alliances before this possible third Sino-Japanese war. We saw similar activities before World War II.

Nevertheless, each party is busy calculating the chance of a third Sino-Japanese war, and weighing the balance.

2.1 CHINA

We could consider that the current China is absolutely at her historical peak if we look back at Chinese history, or we could also consider that China has just passed her historical peak if we compare China with other world powers at this moment [5]. However, our feeling would generally lag the historical process. Almost all the Chinese people feel that China will soon be the world power although no one clearly defines what a world power should do in this respect.

On the surface, China needs the third Sino-Japanese war because Chinese society currently lacks a joined force, which wants to make China better, while every Chinaman thinks of her/himself rather than China.

With the bright prospect that China will soon become a world power, the feeling of throwing away the old pains and humiliations, which mark the unhappy contemporary Chinese history, is becoming strong and stronger in most Chinese minds.

Over recent years, the super-nationalists inside China strongly advocate the conflicts with Japan, and the Internet bloggers advocate the war between China and Japan. This advocated war would be the third Sino-Japanese war if it would occur. This group of people would be the strongest group of interest inside China, who need the third Sino-Japanese war. This is so because they simply hate Japan very much and they are not afraid of Japan and war. With China's fast economic development, these super-nationalists feel that it is time that China can revenge herself of the Japanese aggression into China during the second Sino-Japanese war as well as the humiliation brought by the defeat of China during the first Sino-Japanese war. In fact, most super-nationalists come from grassroots, thus it is no doubt that they love China very much. However, their intention to make a war is mainly based on their feeling. On the other hand, one cannot exclude the possibility that some super-nationalists do not come from grassroots; they might have a good position in Chinese politics. Politically, it is the safest way for anyone else inside China to take a strong position against Japan because no one will accuse a Chinaman to take such an anti-Japan position.

Still, there are many warlike people inside China, whose amount should not be underestimated. Various war affairs in Chinese and international media, films and TV programs impress and inspire this group of people, who really hope to see a war, and the possibility of a third Sino-Japanese war is a popular topic for them.

With the help of Chinese media, the super-nationalists and warlike people are confident that China will certainly defeat Japan easily in any incoming war between China and Japan, even defeat the US easily in any incoming war between China and the US.

Actually, the super-nationalists and warlike people get strong support from ordinary Chinese people and the Chinese media, although the view that super-nationalists and warlike people take does not consider how much China would benefit from the third Sino-Japanese war, and how much China would lose during the third Sino-Japanese war. Naturally, they also do not consider any detailed process in conducting such a war.

In principle, the super-nationalists and warlike people do not have many efficient means to influence the Chinese policy. This is so because the Chinese super-nationalists and warlike people have not organized any meaningful political organizations yet, so they cannot systematically affect the Chinese policy in general. However, at this stage, the Chinese media plays a leading role to promote the possible third Sino-Japanese war, because the moneymaking mechanism requires all Chinese media to report something new and exacting without respect to real facts. Although the Chinese media is patriotic, the mechanism of moneymaking plays a leading role in Chinese media and society. After consistent years of reporting money and sex, more and more audiences have become less and less interested in what is reported by the Chinese media. Therefore the Chinese media needs to attract an audience to make money. The reporting of anti-Japanese sentiment and the enlarging of Chinese military strength are the safest way to run a media. Under these circumstances, the Chinese media is very irresponsible on what they report, therefore their reports are full of illusion on the Chinese military might, which in turn increases the Chinese people's confidence on the outcome of the third Sino-Japanese war.

However, it is not clear whether the Chinese government really hopes the third Sino-Japanese war is a way to make China to become a world power or Pacific Empire, not only because the term of this administration will soon finish, but more importantly the Chinese government has more important issues related to economic development to deal with. However, we must realize that the anti-Japan sentiment is a way to unite the Chinese people, because nowadays Marxism, Maoism and socialism can no longer unite the Chinese people, and no religions can unite the Chinese people either. From this point of view, the Chinese government at worst would not discourage the anti-Japan sentiments inside China. It is certain that Chinese government would get more support from the Chinese people if the Chinese government would take a strong position against Japan.

On the other hand, since the end of Olympic games in Beijing, China, in 2008, China has step-by-step begun to lose her position of international focus; even the Chinese economy has shown some sign of slowdown. Actually, the fast development in the Chinese economy no longer excites the world. The feeling that China is worthy of getting intentional attention could encourage the Chinese government to take a strong position against Japan.

Another fact, which could be an important way to promote the third Sino-Japanese war in the future, is that more and more problems progressively appear in Chinese society. This is leading more and more Chinese people unsatisfied and leading to social unrest. Thus, the promotion of a third Sino-Japanese war would be a way to remove the Chinese people's attention away from various problems inside China.

In some sense, the Chinese army needs the third Sino-Japanese war because the economic development marginalizes the Chinese army's role in modern Chinese society. Since launching various space programs, the Chinese army has more ambitions but little place to exercise these ambitions.

The forces inside China for the power struggle might need the third Sino-Japanese war, because this is the easiest way to find losers in order to defeat their opponents. Actually, this should not be limited to the Chinese political establishments, but any groups of interests, i.e. politicians need the third Sino-Japanese war.

Under these circumstances, China appears to need the third Sino-Japanese war.

Clearly, the arguments listed above do not come from the China's world strategy, because they do not consider the benefit and loss that China will get during and after the third Sino-Japanese war. We should ask ourselves, the

Chinese people, whether China's international interests and strategies require the Chinese people to have a third Sino-Japanese war or whether our feelings and emotions require the Chinese people to have a third Sino-Japanese war? We should ask where a third Sino-Japanese war would lead the Chinese people..

Scientifically, we, the Chinese people, have not yet defined where and how the Chinese interests would collide with the Japanese interests, and whether these collisions would be worthy a war.

2.2 OVERSEA CHINESE

Another strong group of people, who earnestly hope for the third Sino-Japanese war, would be the people, who are against the Chinese government. These people are mostly living oversea but mainly based in the US.

These oversea Chinese people generally love China and hope for a strong and prosperous China, but are unhappy with China's policies. Of course, most of these Chinese people hate Japan too because of the previous Sino-Japanese wars.

It is well known in any country that anti-government organizations hope for war, which will shaken and weaken the government and leave room for the anti-government organization to be active, to have a say, to have a seat in the government, and eventually overthrow the government. For example, the Russian anti-government forces supported the Japanese during the Russo-Japanese war in order to weaken the Russian Empire. On the other hand, the Japanese government was very happy to provide money to support the Russian anti-government forces.

The anti-Chinese government organizations could fully support the third Sino-Japanese war because this is the safest political position. They would clearly benefit from a third Sino-Japanese war no matter whether China or Japan would win. If China would win, these anti-Chinese government organizations would have sincerely supported the third Sino-Japanese war, and most Chinese people would feel them patriotic, and these anti-government organizations would have the chance to enter the Chinese government. If Japan would win, these anti-Chinese government organizations would be happy to see the collapse of the current Chinese government, thus they would have the chance either to enter the new government or even form their own governments because all the Chinese people would have seen how they love China during the third Sino-Japanese war.

Therefore, any consequence of a third Sino-Japanese war would create a win-win situation to favor the anti-Chinese government organizations. Hence they need the war.

The means that Chinese people overseas can take to promote the third Sino-Japanese war would be overseas campaigns to increase the tension between China and Japan. For example, the oversea Chinese sent emails to call for the boycotting of Japanese goods, and so on.

In general, the oversea Chinese's view would not weigh much on the Chinese government policy unless some famous and prominent oversea Chinese people have the chance to exchange their ideas and could influence the Chinese policymakers.

However, the Chinese people overseas indeed have the possibility to influence the Chinese media, which in turn would influence the Chinese policymakers.

An extremely important fact is that neither the Chinese people living in Mainland China nor the Chinese people living overseas have proposed a full and whole picture on the conflicts between China and Japan, and on the third Sino-Japanese war. This is understandable because their life is usually far away from military establishments, far away from military strategic planning, far away from policymaking, and even far away from international affairs. In this sense, the rationale from Chinese people overseas could appear less convincing for a third Sino-Japanese war, because their view and rationale do not include the details on what China will get as well as what China will lose during the war although the oversea Chinese people and political dissidents need the third Sino-Japanese war.

2.3 TAIWAN

Although Taiwan appears to stand along with Mainland China when any dispute occurs between China and Japan, actually Taiwan would benefit dramatically from a third Sino-Japanese war, even from the possible prediction of a third Sino-Japanese war.

First, it is certain that Taiwan will not be involved in any armed conflict between China and Japan, because both are enemies to Taiwan either from ideology or from history. Consequently, Taiwan would be very likely to enjoy her neutral position although her media might take a strong position against Japan, and morally support Mainland China with donated money from ordinary Taiwanese. In this context, the media in both Taiwan and Hong Kong would play an important role in promoting a third Sino-Japanese war; the so-called patriotism for the people living in Taiwan and Hong Kong goes out mainly through the media as well as donated money from some volunteers.

Second, the security treaty between US and Taiwan will guarantee Taiwan's safety, which allows Taiwan to take a neutral position. In this sense, Taiwan is unlikely to launch any attack on Japanese soil, even on Japanese interests overseas if we consider the small size of Taiwanese troops. Of course, Japan would not attack Taiwan anyway because Taiwan lost her strategic significance since the end of World War II, during which the Japanese air force could use Taiwan as airbase to bombard the Mainland China.

Third, Taiwan will benefit no matter whether China defeats Japan or Japan defeats China. With her neutral position, Taiwan can theoretically make money from both China and Japan during the third Sino-Japanese war by supplying necessary materials.

Fourth, no one could exclude the possibility that Taiwan would declare her independence during the third Sino-Japanese war.

Fifth, any increase of tension between China and Japan would be almost useful to Taiwan because her tension with Mainland China would be reduced either in relative comparison or absolute comparison with the increase of tension between China and Japan.

So theoretically, Taiwan needs the third Sino-Japanese war, even Hong Kong could benefit from the third Sino-Japanese war. This is so simply because they do not need to consider whether China will win or lose during the third Sino-Japanese war. Literally, both Taiwan and Hong Kong would adopt the position to promote the war between China and Japan.

2.4 JAPAN

The current political and economic atmosphere would support the Japanese government taking a strong position against China, simply because Japan would not like to see China becoming a dominant force in the western part of Pacific Rim. This would perhaps hurt Japanese pride, but it is difficult to judge whether China's influence would hurt the Japanese because currently we have no way to define Japanese interests, which collide with the Chinese interests.

Actually, whether the extension of China's influence could pose threats to Japanese interests is a trivial issue. The real issue would be that Japan should defeat China if she wants to be a dominant force in western Pacific Ocean.

The tension between China and Japan will give a best pretext for the rearming of Japan and for amending the Japanese constitution. Actually, the Japanese economy has run into a deadlock for years, and very likely no new Japanese government would find a good and great solution to her economy. Politically, no new Japanese government seems to find a new way to enhance the Japanese position on an international platform and it still seems far away for Japan to become a permanent member in the UN Security Council.

This is indeed quite normal, because the many current international bodies were designed and established based on the consequences of World War II. No major world powers would like to see any change in this "world order". Arguably the aim of changing world order was the pretext for World War II, which Japan had actively attended and furiously advocated the new order in Asia.

All the unhappiness in Japan would easily lead Japan to become either aggressive or low-spirited, however the current competition for world market would not allow a low-spirited Japan to exist. On the other hand, perhaps a thinkable solution for Japanese economy would be rearming of Japan.

The Japanese government could promote a third Sino-Japanese war by adopting an increasingly stronger position against China.

2.5 NORTH KOREA

From each and every aspect, North Korea needs the third Sino-Japanese war desperately. This is very simple because in any case North Korea always has the intention to wage a war either in the near or the remote future with South Korea as well as the alliance of South Korea in order to unify Korea. North Korea has been preparing this unification war for several decades, however one of the fears in North Korean leaders' mind is that North Korea is not sure whether China would be fully supportive in terms of army and weaponries if the unification war would occur. Therefore the third Sino-Japanese war would formally and officially put China and North Korea into the same boat, even the tension between China and Japan would push China to stand more closely with North Korea.

If the above analysis would be the best for North Korean interests, then the next question would be whether North Korea would be able to promote the third Sino-Japanese war? If so, what means would North Korea use to promote the third Sino-Japanese war?

Theoretically and practically, North Korea has little influence either on Chinese leaders or on Chinese people, because China in fact has more interests in South Korea rather than North Korea. This is so because the Chinese leaders consider international affairs mainly from viewpoint of economic development while nowadays the Chinese people generally view a country mainly based on whether the country in question is poor or rich.

However, North Korea would still have several ways to promote the possible third Sino-Japanese war: (i) to be more and more proactive in raising the tension between North Korea and South Korea; (ii) to be more and more hostile to the Japanese government; (iii) to be more and more hostile to the US government; and (iv) to go through a secret way to provoke the third Sino-Japanese war (Chapter 5 Provoked War).

Now let us look at the scenarios from North Korea viewpoint. If the third Sino-Japanese war would occur but not spread into North Korea, it would be the best scenario for North Korea. Even we could say that this type of war would be a once-in-history opportunity for North Korea, even for both North and South Koreas. This is so because Korea could not keep her independence and territory free from the first Sino-Japanese war, the Russo-Japanese war and the second Sino-Japanese war. However, we could not think out what North Korea or South Korea would like to use this once-in-history opportunity to do. However, this opportunity would still be possible because the US and South Korea's mutual treaty guarantees the safety of South Korea, therefore Japan might not need to adopt the same approach as the Japanese army did in all previous wars to go through Korea to reach China.

On the other hand, if the third Sino-Japanese war would spread to Korea, the damage to South Korea might be larger than to North Korea, because South Korea might become the target of Chinese force. This would be a good scenario for North Korea too.

In both circumstances, we hardly find any reason that would lead North Korea to go against the third Sino-Japanese war.

2.6 SOUTH KOREA

Actually, South Korea also needs the third Sino-Japanese war, because this war is unlikely to lead to any direct attack on South Korea soil if the Chinese force would be immediately silenced. In such a case, North Korea would not dare initiate any attack on South Korea, while a militarily silenced China would not support North Korea, then the only consequence is more likely to be the collapse of North Korea.

On the other hand, Japan is so close to China that Japan and her alliances would have no need to use any military facilities in South Korea to attack China. If this would be the case, South Korea could be in a somewhat neutral position in the third Sino-Japanese war without any damage to her soil. Can we not say this would be the best circumstance for South Korea? This is also because any rebuilding of China and Japan after the third Sino-Japanese war would provide an unprecedented opportunity for South Korea's industry.

In this view, South Korea would adopt a position to indirectly promote the war. On the other hand, South Korea in some sense is a model for most Chinese people to follow because of her cultural influence as well as the influence of products from South Korea. Therefore, the people from South Korea could influence the Chinese view to a very large degree, for example, the email I received from an oversea Chinese says that the South Korean people never buy Japanese goods, so the Chinese people should learn from South Korean people and never buy Japanese goods. No matter whether this statement is true or false and whether this statement goes against WTO agreements, this statement would promote the trading war between China and Japan, increase the tension between China and Japan, and encourage the Chinese people to buy South Korean goods.

2.7 RUSSIA

Although Russia has been progressively becoming powerful in terms of her economy and her military might once again, Russia has less and less interests in international affairs. The focus of the Russian government and the Russian people concentrates more and more on narrow interests, as do the Chinese people. This means that Russia is gradually returning to the time of Russia Empire, i.e. we only need to consider Russia as a regional power rather than world power, even an isolated power that can effectively but inefficiently defend herself but has no interests beyond Russian borders.

To a certain degree, Russia would therefore take a neutral position towards the current disputes between China and Japan, i.e. Russia would neither promote nor discourage the third Sino-Japanese on the surface.

However, the third Sino-Japanese war would certainly be a gift to Russia, because such a war would weaken both China and Japan. As Russia has occupied the Japanese islands since the end of World War II and the Sino-Russian border has not yet been settled, the third Sino-Japanese war would be good for Russia. As a full-scale third Sino-Japanese war would provoke the war between China and Japanese alliance, Russia would be happy to see the consumption of US and NATO in this terrible war if Russia would efficiently and effectively keep herself away from the third Sino-Japanese war but rearm herself under the pretext of third Sino-Japanese war.

Likely, the current Russia has little influence either on China or on Japan, thus Russia could not do much to promote the third Sino-Japanese war. However, the real point in promoting the war is that Russia could become a major supplier for weaponry to the Chinese army. Any arms race in this region would certainly benefit Russian industry.

If the tension between China and Japan spreads to Southeast Asia, we could not exclude the possibility that Russia would once again have new ambitions to return to Southeast Asia, and even join the arms race in that part of Pacific Rim.

Russia needs the third Sino-Japanese war, because Russia would become a Pacific Empire in this part of Pacific Rim since both China and Japan should be heavily damaged during the third Sino-Japanese war.

2.8 INDIA

Another player to consider is India. Although India currently is a silent player in various disagreements and disputes between China and Japan, India is a serious competitor with China in the sense of economy and influence on Asia, especially South Asia. With the fast development of the Indian economy, India would have more to say about international affairs. Still, with the rapid increase of the Indian population, India will soon pass China to become the country with the largest population in the world. Both these issues will soon lead India to become a permanent member of UN Security Council. At such time, India would play a vital role to promote or stop the third Sino-Japanese war because China would not expect to get much support from the UN Security Council simply because the US, UK and France would be in line with Japan, while Russia would be more likely to take a neutral position. Thus, the Indian position would be extremely important.

Certainly, the position China now holds would be somewhat different if India becomes the country with the largest population and huge economic power.

Honestly and frankly, the relationship between China and India is not good, although leaders in both countries pretend that there is a good relationship between the two countries.

It is hard to define at this moment what benefit India will get from the third Sino-Japanese war. However, this would not be the case if India would join the world alliance with Japan to defeat China. This is so because any treaty signed after the third Sino-Japanese war would give the direct involvers some benefit. For India, it seems that India will settle her disputes along borders between China and India forever; of course this would be the minimal achievement for India if she would take part in the war.

Still, China seems to have a closer relationship with India's number one enemy, Pakistan, thus if China would be defeated in the third Sino-Japanese war,

Pakistan would be weaker than she is now. From this viewpoint, India will gain tremendously from the third Sino-Japanese war. If we expand our view furthermore, who can say that India would not be the number one world power after China, Japan, US and NATO are weakened too much in the third Sino-Japanese war.

Although India needs the third Sino-Japanese war, she does not seem to have many ways to promote this war because Indians have little influence on Chinese and Japanese policymaking. Indian media has almost no influence on Chinese media.

2.9 US

To exhaust our imaginations, we could not find any reason why the US would not need the third Sino-Japanese war. So the US needs the third Sino-Japanese war from almost every point of view. This is very simple because the competition between China and Japan is the competition to become a Pacific Empire. This Pacific Empire will eventually challenge the current Pacific and Atlantic Empire, the United States of America.

Among various groups of interest hoping for the third Sino-Japanese war, the US army would want this war. The US army will soon be completely free from Iraq and Afghanistan, so the US troops need to find some hotspots in the world to be involved in. Practically, the US troops are most experienced troops in the world because the US troops never stopped fighting since the end of World War II. They need various scales of war in order to increase and refresh their experience. Thus third Sino-Japanese war would provide a rare opportunity for training US troops.

On the other hand, the third Sino-Japanese war would be a great gift to the US because the US, as she did during World War I and World War II, would be happy to see other world powers and regional powers kill each other mercilessly without consuming too many American lives until the last moment, when the US would involve herself to play a decisive role.

The third Sino-Japanese war would weaken both China and Japan; both China and Japan might need years to fully recover. In such a case, the US would enjoy her superior position for the rest of the 21st century.

Still, the US needs the third Sino-Japanese war because currently China is the only country supporting North Korea. It is almost certain that China would be defeated during the third Sino-Japanese war with the involvement of other world powers, and then North Korea would be silent forever. However, the question raised here is whether it is worth having the third Sino-Japanese war to silence North Korea? This solution does not seem cost-effective.

So how can the US promote the third Sino-Japanese war? The simplest way is to allow Japan to rearm herself, to allow Japan to amend her constitution, to strengthen the military tie between Japan and the US and between South Korea and the US. Another way is to support the Chinese people who are living in the US, because this group of Chinese people sometimes has a strong influence on Chinese policymaking as the most powerful lobby group.

Actually the US, as the only power in the world, has much an interest in promoting the third Sino-Japanese war. As a simple example, the US can block any resolution related to disputes and disagreements between China and Japan from being passed by any international body.

2.10 UK AND NATO

Actually, the UK and NATO would simply follow the US anywhere the US goes. In this context, the UK and NATO need the third Sino-Japanese war.

To a very small degree, the British army might want to join a war. We have seen that British troops have been involved in most conflicts in the world since the British army has had the capacity to wage a war beyond their border. As a recent example, the number of involvements of the British army in conflicts under Tony Blair's government is a record in British history.

On the other hand, it is hard to elaborate other concrete reasons for the UK and NATO to desperately hope for the third Sino-Japanese war, because this war would be so far away from NATO countries, from their interests and very costly. Still we cannot see any direct benefit that NATO countries would get during the third Sino-Japanese war because NATO countries cannot be a weapon supplier to China while the US supplied weapons are sufficient for Japan. On the other hand, many NATO countries currently are far less ambitious than they were a century before.

It would be questionable whether the UK and NATO would promote the third Sino-Japanese war although they might be more interested in promoting a cold war between China and Japan, for example, a trading war. To some degree, the UK government could possibly influence Chinese policymakers because of her previous empire position in the world. Many Chinese scholars, whose views weigh on Chinese policymaking, would follow the US and UK suggestions closely and faithfully without any elaborations and considerations.

2.11 ISLAMISM

Although the Islam world is far away from the western part of the Pacific Rim, and far away from China and Japan, and people in the Islam world are far less interested in any potential war between China and Japan. Any clear mind would easily figure out that the third Sino-Japanese war would be potentially good for the Islam world, and actually Islamism.

Someone once suggested that Islamism would prevail around the world, which would be possible even without looking at various events, which have occurred since the beginning of the 21st century. The full capacity of capitalism seems to have run out, and there are indeed no other powerful ideologies to compete with Islamism or replace capitalism.

Naturally, we should realize and admit that Islamism, itself, would have great difficulty prevailing over the world, however the third Sino-Japanese war would provide a precious opportunity.

This argument is very reasonable because the very high tension between China and Japan would draw the attention from almost all the world, thus pressure on the Islam world would be substantially reduced. If the third Sino-Japanese war would really happen, then the US and NATO would be actively involved in various negotiations, and even military activities, supporting Japan to defeat China. The Islam world would feel much relieved. No world power would care a nuclear program in any Islam country. The pressure from the US and Europe on the Islamic world would be sharply reduced.

Immediately after the end of World War II, many Islam countries drove colonialism out from their countries in Asia and Africa under cover of Marxism and Leninism. Since then, Islam countries began to drive dictatorship out from their countries as we have seen in North Africa. How can we imagine the world to be if the third Sino-Japanese war occurs followed by World War III?

Frankly, the current Islam world has little consideration on the third Sino-Japanese war therefore the Islam world would not calculate too much profit from this war.

Arguably, the third Sino-Japanese war would be a great opportunity for Iran and Turkey to quietly reach their goals without disturbance.

On the other hand, the Islamic world has little influence to promote the third Sino-Japanese war besides observing the process of increasing tension between China and Japan.

2.12 WORLD INDUSTRY AND BANKERS

Arguably, World War II largely occurred after the popularity of the personal car. In this sense, no one knows what products would once again be as popular as car, TV, personal computer and mobile phones, and what products would once again make as much money as these products.

Certainly, if the world industry cannot find a popular civilian product, which would be as popular as TV, computers, and mobile phones, then the option to rearm Japan, and create a new arms race would be on the table.

Once again, one of the main reasons that led the world to come out from the Great Depression in the 1920s and 1930s, could be attributed to the rearming of Europe. Therefore, Europe felt far less pain than the US during Great Depression, because the rearming of the US was not on the agenda.

Currently and actually, Japan would be the country that most desperately needs to find a way to drag itself out from her decade-long recession, for which the politicians do not have any reliable remedy. Therefore, the rearming of Japan would definitely be an option for Japanese and world industries. If the furious arms race can be initiated in the western Pacific Ocean and the western part of the Pacific Rim, then the sales orders would be enough for world industries to work for decades.

On the other hand, bankers now desperately need to find a place to lend their money, and the lessons in property investment will not allow the bankers to risk themselves again, so the best place to lend money would be the arms industry, which is guaranteed by governments.

In these contexts, we would say that the world industries and bankers need the third Sino-Japanese war. As the world industries and bankers have sufficient money to lobby politicians and lawmakers, it would not be difficult for them to promote the arms race in the western Pacific Ocean and the western part of Pacific Rim.

Technically and practically, there is great need of a new generation of weaponry if we project that the third Sino-Japanese war might occur at the time that no more oil would be available. The weaponry required during an oil shortage era would completely reshape the world industries and provide an unprecedented opportunity for world industries because armies around the world need to change their weaponry.

Chapter 3

WORLD BEFORE THE THIRD
SINO-JAPANESE WAR

and in that interval nature had been busy in selecting her new favored class.
— Brooks Adams, The Theory of Social Revolutions [7]

The analysis in the previous chapter suggests that almost all the world might need the third Sino-Japanese war, thus we should have some concept of our world before the third Sino-Japanese war, i.e. we must have an estimation of the world powers, world orders, world organizations, and so on and before entering the further analysis on the third Sino-Japanese war that, although could be planned and designed now, would be conducted in the future according to the future situation rather than the current situation.

Let us assume that the third Sino-Japanese war would possibly occur within the next 20- or 30- or 50-, even 100-year period, which would be more likely to be a task for the next generation, or even the next, next generation to wage the war. However, we need to have a somewhat clearer picture on the whole world for the next 20- or 30- or 50-, even 100-year period in order to discuss the third Sino-Japanese war because this war would certainly be related to not only the western part of the Pacific Rim but also the world. In this frame, we should now imagine how the world powers, world orders, world organizations, etc. would be over the next 50 years.

However, in some sense, the future is so far from now, it appears obscure so it would be difficult to determine the groups of interest who would still need the third Sino-Japanese war.

3.1 US

Perhaps, we need at first to look at the current Atlantic and Pacific Empire, the US, before looking at the UN for the next 20-, 30-, 50-year period. In my previous book [5], I used the results from the Lanchaster's equation to estimate a country's domination in world affairs. From an economic view, a country's GDP would be 26.1%, 41.7% and 73.9% of world GDP in order to lead, dominate and control the world economy. The US GDP accounts for about 25% of world GDP at this moment, while the half-life for the decay of ratio of US GDP versus world GDP is about 50 to 60 years if we consider that the US GDP was about half of world GDP immediately after World War II. Accordingly, the US economy decayed from a dominated position to a lead position from the middle of the 20th century to the beginning of the 21st century. According to the half-life of decaying proportion of US GDP versus world GDP, the US would contribute about 12% of world GDP around the middle of the 21st century, which means that the US would not lead the world economy. Naturally, the contribution of US military power to the world would decay with the decay of contributions from the US economy to the world economy.

Another issue, which should be considered, is that the American-invented so-called outsourcing would sooner or later de-industrialize the US, even her western allies as well. This might simply suggest that the US someday would not have sufficient war industries to produce warplanes and warships, even the US would need to buy warplanes and warships from other countries, which perhaps would be the point of collapse of the US Empire.

Following that, perhaps, we could give a similar estimation for the US role in the political affairs on the world stage. Accordingly we would have different views on the US' role in the future.

If we consider that the US would be a troublemaker, then the US would make fewer troubles with the decay of her economic power. Can we assume that the world would be more peaceful with less intervention from the US? In some sense, the answer would be Yes, however another answer would be No. The explanation for the latter answer is that currently the security treaties with US in many countries maintain these countries' safety. With the inevitable decay of the US role worldwide, many treaties should physically die, and then new hot spots would appear.

If we would not consider the US as a troublemaker, then world peace could become more and more difficult to maintain for another half a century, and more and more wars would likely occur because of the decaying of the US Empire.

So one thing seems to be sure; with the decay of the US Empire, the world would soon or late enter a very unstable phase, and we would expect to see more armed conflicts.

3.2 UN AND ITS SECURITY COUNCIL

At first, we may need to imagine the structure of the UN for the next 20- or 30- or 50-year period, This imagination is important because if the UN still exists for the next half a century then it would mean that the world order would not have changed significantly because a world-scale war would be the pre-condition to demolish the current UN although the UN is becoming more and more insignificant, hopeless and concentrating her efforts on impossible but sometimes trivial issues such as road safety, influenza, etc., because the UN cannot pass any meaningful and significant resolution. Practically and technically, various groups of interest are rapidly replacing the role of the UN such as G-7, G-20, and so on. However, no matter how weak and unimportant the UN would be, Japan, India, Germany, Brazil, African countries, and perhaps other countries, would desperately try to become permanent members in the UN Security Council. If this would be the case, one would not expect to see the UN pass any meaningful and significant resolutions because the composition of Security Council fully represents groups of different interest, and each has the power to veto any meaningful resolution.

Under this circumstance, the UN will not make any meaningful and significant resolution if Japan would like to rearm herself or if the third Sino-Japanese war occurs.

No matter whether the third Sino-Japanese war occurs or not, Japan would have a chance to become a permanent member of the UN Security Council. This is so because Japan is a relatively active member in the UN, but more importantly because Japan could get the support from almost all of the industrialized countries. Therefore, whether Japan would become a permanent member in the UN Security Council it will depend on whether the UN will significantly reform to such a degree that China's veto would not minimize the chance that Japan will become a permanent member of the UN Security Council.

On the other hand, it is very doubtful whether China would use her veto power to block Japan from becoming a permanent member in the UN Security Council, not only because China rarely uses her veto power in the UN but also because China would consider whether her veto would furthermore worsen the relationship between China and Japan.

However, if Japan would become a permanent member in the UN Security Council, we would expect that Japan would not veto anything else in-line with the US. This would be the similar case for China. However, the real point would be that either China or Japan would have the probability to kill any resolution related to themselves to make the UN furthermore lose her credits.

Frankly India would have a bigger chance than Japan to become a permanent member of the UN Security Council. We would expect that India would adopt a slightly neutral position in various disputes and disagreements between China and Japan, but would have a trend to support Japan.

Actually, no matter of which country would become a permanent member in the UN Security Council, China would become more and more isolated in the UN Security Council because China does not have many allies, not even allies in the UN Security Council.

3.3 REARMING OF JAPAN

Japan will certainly prepare once again to become a real Pacific Empire [8], so the question here is whether Japan needs to rearm herself before the third Sino-Japanese war because the Japanese constitution prohibits the rearming of Japan. So does Japan need to amend her constitution first?

The real question raised here is whether the US allows the rearming of Japan: is it opening a Pandora's box? The US government frequently opens various Pandora's boxes for her provisional interests, and then spends more resources to undo them.

If the US will agree that Japan can rearm herself, then the next question would be how long will Japan need to rearm herself? Human history might suggest that it may take ten to twenty years to rearm a country. In such case, Japan at first needs a whole new generation, who have the will to fight for the Pacific Empire. With the current low birth rate in Japan, one would wonder whether Japan could create such a warlike generation?

Moreover, the surrounding countries would not sit quietly and silently to see the rearming of Japan. This means that Japan needs to beat other countries in a new round of arms race. This race would be different from the arming of Japan before World War II when most Asian countries were in feudal societies or were colonized and had no industry.

A further question is to which degree Japan needs to rearm herself, and to which extent would the US allow Japan to rearm? This is so because the Japanese ambition would not increase proportionally to her degree of rearming, but increase faster than the speed of rearming of Japan. Thus would Japan become a threat to US interests when the Japanese army becomes too strong with stronger ambition?

Consequently, the next question is whether East Asian and Southeast Asian countries would be happy with the rearming of Japan? Then who can guarantee the safety of these Southeast Asian countries and persuade them not to arm themselves.

Still, will East Asian and Southeast Asian countries have enough power to prevent the rearming of Japan at the UN?

Meanwhile, one might ask whether Japan would have a need to rearm herself to initiate third Sino-Japanese war? Of course the most serious question is whether Japan would need nuclear weapons?

Another question is whether a new arms race will be triggered in this region; if Japan rearms herself will China and Russia rearm themselves?

Without definite answers to these questions, it would be very difficult for Japan to rearm herself without alarming almost all the East and Southeast Asian countries.

3.4 RUSSIA'S STRENGTH

If the contribution of the US to world GDP and military power decays along the pathway over last 50 years, then we should look at another former superpower, Russia. Could Russia once again become ambitious?

In principle, the Russian economy would continue increasing because she at least has sufficient raw materials, which would be the best bargaining factor in the 21st century. Still the strength of the market economy would eventually push Russia into the front of the world economy.

In such case, three equally powerful players, China, Japan and Russia, would appear in the western Pacific Ocean while the US might no longer be very interested in the western Pacific with her decaying economy and military power over the next 50 years. Then, which country would dominate the western Pacific Ocean? Very much likely, these three countries would share the same dream and form the Pacific Empire together. That is to say neither China, nor Japan, nor Russia would become the Pacific Empire because of the counterbalance among these three countries.

However, this does not mean that a strong Russia would be necessary to prevent the occurrence of third Sino-Japanese war. Practically, Russia would still focus on Europe as she traditionally did, but would secretly hope for the occurrence of a third Sino-Japanese war, and it would be far greater for Russia if nuclear weapons were not used in the third Sino-Japanese war.

On the other hand, a second Russo-Japanese war is totally unlikely because Russia needs to consume herself rather than sit to see the fighting between China and Japan; then Russia would eventually and naturally become the Pacific Empire.

3.5. INDIA

It is a matter of time, within the next 50 years, before India will enter into the rank of world power. As the Indian population will certainly surpass the Chinese population, it will depend on Indian economic strength whether India's international position would surpass China's international position.

If both the Indian population and economy would surpass China, then China would not be able to draw more attention from the world as she does at present. Meanwhile, India would become more aggressive and bold, as we have seen her intervention in Sri Lanka.

A serious question raised here is whether India's interests would collide with China's interests, with the US' interests and with Japan's interests. If India would behave as a world power, then the tension between China and Japan might be reduced because of the new structure of power in South Asia.

If India would become a world power, then we should ask whether Pakistan would submit to India? If so, we would expect to see an India Empire in the Indian Ocean. If so, the strategy on the whole world would be changed because the Indian Ocean would perhaps be the busiest ocean due to the transport of raw materials from Africa to other parts of the world while India dominates it.

Of course, the next fifty years would provide India with unimaginably great opportunity.

3.6 EUROPEAN UNION AND NATO

The most powerful international military organization would still be NATO, which can do anything regardless of the UN. However, the future of NATO would closely be related to how many countries will join NATO in the next 20-, 30- or 50-year period, i.e. the NATO expansion. Could Russia join the NATO? Could Japan join NATO although Japan is located far away from the North Atlantic

Ocean? Could South Korea join NATO in order to balance the threat from North Korea?

Still, one should ask whether the European Union would become more powerful than NATO due the decay of the US? In that case, one would say that the EU would not be equivalent to NATO. What political role would the European Union play if the European Union would become stronger than now? Could the European Union behave in the UN as an independent bloc? Would the European Union get a seat in the UN Security Council as a permanent member? This could be possible because the USSR was theoretically composed of fifteen republics but was a permanent member of the UN Security Council.

3.7 CRUDE OIL

An extremely important consideration would be that crude oil could perhaps become rare, and rarer, before the occurrence of third Sino-Japanese war. This would produce a profound influence on political, economic, even military structures around the world.

Then, the currently silent forces with rich oil resources would have more to say. This force perhaps will reshape the world and change the face of the world. The question here is whether an oil-shortage era would reduce the tension between China and Japan? However, this also could be a strong pretext for the third Sino-Japanese war because of the potential oil resources in the disputed sea. Thus, it could be more likely that the tension would increase proportionally to the degree of oil shortage around the world.

3.8 BRAZIL

Frankly and honestly, Brazil currently does not play any important role in the disputes and disagreements between China and Japan. However, Brazil could become more important. The Brazilian strategic role could soon go beyond her border. Could Brazil create a South Atlantic Treaty Organization together with South Africa to share their domination on South Atlantic Ocean?

In such a case, the US would certainly have less and less influence on the western Pacific Ocean, so China would feel less worried about whether the US would immediately and unconditionally support Japan if the tension between China and Japan increases beyond the limit.

3.9 TWO KOREAS

As our view projects for the next half a century, and even a century, a question raised here is whether the two Koreas would unite in the foreseeing future. Under the current world order established after World War II, there is no possibility that two Koreas would unite without heavy bloodshed.

This means that we would still see two Koreas over the next half a century, which perhaps would create a record in human history that a single-national country is divided for so long without a solution. In this projected case, both Koreas would be separated for a century.

This is a clear example that national interest subdues the ideological difference, subdues international pressure and subdues economic interests.

On the other hand, if both Koreas would unite, the situation in East Asia would be totally different than it is now. This would be so because the new united Korea would have nuclear weapons and sophisticated modern technologies. Considering Korean history, it would be doubtless that the new Korea would hold a boldly hostile view against Japan.

There would be a power balance or unbalance in East Asia. Clearly the only answer to this situation for Japan would be a large-scale rearming with nuclear weapons. We would expect to see a full-scale arms race in East Asia.

However, this situation would be very unlikely because the world order would not be changed without the collapse of old world powers.

3.10 CHINA

A similar situation would hold for China, i.e. China and Taiwan would not unite under the current atmosphere, which would also be a record in human history because it seems that not many countries have been divided for so long without hope of uniting.

In general, China is a nation used to her own pathway. This means that the Chinese people would still hate the Japanese people for the sake of a second Sino-Japanese war. Perhaps, China would take a strong and stronger position against Japan as both countries pursue to become the Pacific Empire.

However, it is still not clear whether China would take an extremely strong position against Japan and go to a third Sino-Japanese war.

Chapter 4

CAN WE AVOID THE THIRD SINO-JAPANESE WAR?

> Anger may in time change to gladness; vexation may be succeeded by content. But a kingdom that has once been destroyed can never come again into being; nor can the dead ever be brought back to life. Hence the enlightened ruler is heedful, and the good general full of caution. This is the way to keep a country at peace and an army intact.
>
> — Sun Tzu, The Art Of War [9]

The analyses in previous chapters suggest the possibility of occurrence of a third Sino-Japanese war in the future. Then, we should ask whether there would be ways to avoid a third Sino-Japanese war? This question is important because history clearly shows that the outcome of any war might not be identical to what the war designers openly or secretly hoped, thus the outcome of the third Sino-Japanese war might not reach the goal designed by various groups of interests. If so, why should we not do our best to avoid the third Sino-Japanese war? Why should we not do our best to diffuse the tension between China and Japan? Why should we not rally international forces to make more peace deals between China and Japan, and between rivals?

Currently, it seems that neither China nor Japan is interested in cooling the tension between China and Japan, simply because the way to avoid conflicts would affect their ambition of becoming the Pacific Empire. Meanwhile, we cannot see any serious efforts made by the international community to reduce the tension between China and Japan.

Perhaps, we might assume that various parties lack interest to reduce the tensions between China and Japan, or we might assume that various parties lack the methods to reduce these tensions.

4.1 CAN CHINA BUY JAPANESE HEART?

Nowadays, China has plenty of money, which is the pride of China. Accordingly can China use her money to buy the Japanese heart to avoid the third Sino-Japanese war?

This means that China would change her investment focus from the US to Japan in order to create sufficient jobs in Japan rather than to create jobs in North America, Australia, and in other remote places such as Africa. This means that China would buy more Japanese goods than goods from other parts of the world. This eventually means that China has more to say in Japanese politics, and has more influence on Japanese policymaking process. The heavy investments from China might make the Japanese people become much friendlier and less hostile towards China and the Chinese people, so this will step by step change the tone in some Japanese media as well as some Chinese media.

Until now, China's oversea investments focus on raw materials as well as the US market. Thus if China will change her investment focus to Japan, then China would buy US bonds to a far more lesser degree, which would lead to the massive devaluation of the US dollar, and a new round of political pressure from the US government on the Chinese government so that China can continue financing the US government. This approach would also lead the outcry from the American Chinese to ask the Chinese government to continue pouring money into the US on one hand, while the outcry from the super nationalists inside China to stop pouring money into Japan on the other hand.

Politically and economically, this approach would provide the Chinese government with an opportunity to bargain with the US.

Perhaps, one thinkable bargain with the US government would be to reduce US support to Taiwan. This bargain with the US is possible if we consider our assumption of the time of occurrence of the third Sino-Japanese war would be as far as a half a century from now on, and the contribution of China's GDP to the world GDP would continue increasing while the contribution of US' GDP to the world GDP would continue decreasing. In this context, this bargain is most acceptable for the Chinese people.

Another unthinkable bargain, which can even be called blackmail, with the US government would be to ask the US troops to leave South Korea. However, this would endanger all of East Asia, because North Korea might use this Sino-American bargain as a signal to attack South Korea.

Anyway, the switch of Chinese investments from the rest of the world to Japan is an approach to buy the Japanese heart to avoid the third Sino-Japanese war.

Objectively and economically, an approach to buy Japanese hearts might be easier than an approach to buy Americans' heart: (i) Japan has a smaller population than the US, therefore the investment in Japan would create relatively more jobs in population percentage; (ii) the Japanese workforce is small because most Japanese women do not work, therefore the creation of jobs would be mainly related to the Japanese males; (iii) the Japanese currency is more stable than the US dollar, so at least we, the Chinese people, do not need to worry about our valuable investments being devalued as are investments in the US; and (iv) Japan might have a smaller chance than the US to default.

4.2 DEVELOPMENT OF CO-ECONOMY IN EAST ASIA

Another approach would be to further merge the Chinese and Japanese economy together, which could include South Korea. Actually, this is a good way to stabilize East Asia [10]. The East Asia economic bloc would be the biggest bloc in the world other than the North American economic bloc and the European Union bloc, and the most dynamic bloc in the world. This approach would not only reduce the tension between China and Japan, but also reduce the tension between North Korea and South Korea, if China, Japan and South Korea could invest heavily in North Korea.

If Russia could join this proposed East Asia economic bloc with her resources in the western part of the Pacific Rim, then three big, rather equal, players would further stabilize the East Asia region to prevent either a Korean war or a third Sino-Japanese war from happening.

Generally, US policymakers would not be happy about this approach, because this could squeeze the US influence out of East Asia. Thus, each and every effort should be made to find a way to save the face of the US if this approach would be under consideration.

Another worrying player in this East Asia economic bloc would be South Korea, because she might feel that three powerful nations would encircle her. This would leave a way to make the US stay in East Asia. On the other hand, the US might lose her interests in this region due to the decaying of her economic contribution to the world although US policymakers might be willing to do so.

4.3 NON-AGGRESSION TREATY

Currently, a non-aggression pact between China and Japan is impossible. Perhaps one might wonder whether there is a possibility that a non-aggression pact could be signed between China and the US, which would pave the way to sign the non-aggression pact between China and Japan, and even further between China and India as well as other countries.

More importantly, the non-aggression pact between China and Japan would prevent any provoked war (see Chapter 5).

Here a question raised is why the previous Chinese governments including various feudal dynasties did not sign any non-aggression pact between China and Japan, and between China and western powers. Although there could be many answers to this question, perhaps we, the Chinese people, who cannot perceive and recognize an approached danger, are the main reason. This is so simply because we, the Chinese people, fully concentrated on our narrow interests without any sense of international affairs. Historically and actually, almost all the treaties signed by previous Chinese governments were either unfair treaties or humiliating treaties, which we were forced to sign by foreign powers. Very likely, the previous Chinese governments never actively and voluntarily negotiated with foreign powers and signed any non-aggression pact to guarantee the safety of China with respect to her territory and borders and interests. This was a typical isolation for a country with the population size as big as China and with the territorial size as large as China, and this was the fault of our Chinese thoughts because we do not want to understand the world, but consider ourselves great and ancient.

If we consider the Chinese thoughts and behavior in the past, it would be very difficult to sign any non-aggression pact between China and Japan, and between China and the US.

On the other hand, any non-aggression pact between China and Japan should predict the possible territorial and political rearrangements in East Asia. One question is whether North Korea would stand in her current position forever? If both Koreas would be united, then the withdrawal of US troops from East Asia would be expected..Will this change the political and territorial landscape in East Asia? Without such a prediction and elaboration, any war between the two Koreas would annul the non-aggression pact between China and Japan even if we consider the possibility that the Japanese air force might attack the nuclear facility in North Korea.

4.4 EFFECTS OF COMMON CULTURE

Not long ago, ancient Chinese thoughts and ideas became popular inside China, of which our Chinese people are so proud. Many Chinese people even consider that these ancient Chinese thoughts could conquer the world without blood. If so, theoretically, these ancient Chinese thoughts are common culture and common tradition for East Asia and Southeast Asia, especially, for both China and Japan, i.e. China and Japan share a common culture and common tradition.

We could ask whether the re-popularity of ancient Chinese culture and thoughts could provide a chance to buy the Japanese heart in order to make these two countries closer? However, history shows the common culture and common tradition did not prevent the first and second Sino-Japanese wars in the past, so how can we anticipate that our shared common culture and common tradition could prevent the third Sino-Japanese war from happening?

Of course, the re-popularity of ancient Chinese thoughts was directed to the Chinese people, but history has already demonstrated that ancient Chinese thoughts could not defend China, so we would not expect much from our shared common culture and common tradition to reduce the tensions between China and Japan.

4.5 INTERNATIONAL SOLUTION

Until now, there is no intention either in Japan or in China to present their disputes and disagreements to any international body. Of course, the international body has constantly discredited itself so no authority is likely to solve the disputes and disagreements between China and Japan..

Current fashion in conducting a war is not to declare the war officially, so the question left here is whether the international body has any legal solution for this type of war.

Another relevant issue is that both China and Japan are countries that pay high attention to their 'face' values. This creates a dangerous situation, for example, if the Japanese air force would successfully attack the Chinese nuclear facilities, while the 'face-loved' Chinese tradition would not allow China to admit this attack officially. This would be the same as the rumor that the Israeli air force had attacked Syrian nuclear facilities while both Israel and Syria denied this rumor; then what would the international body do?

We therefore argue that the world needs new definitions in order to maintain peace and country's sovereignty. Why wasn't this issue presented to the G-8 meeting?

Chapter 5

PROVOKED WAR

A single spark can start a prairie fire.
— Mao Zedong, A single spark can start a prairie fire. January 5, 1930 [11]

As analyzed in the previous chapters, many countries and groups of interests, if not the whole world, need the third Sino-Japanese war. Consequently, under the current atmosphere the Chinese people and the Japanese people hold more and more negative views against each other.

Thus we should analyze whether a third party can use this rare and important opportunity to induce the third Sino-Japanese war? In this context, both Chinese people and Japanese people should not underestimate such a possibility.

Contemporary history has fully demonstrated such a possibility, as a recent example, we can refer to two countries, Iraq and Afghanistan, whose ruin is due to the attack on the World Trade Center on September 11, 2001. As evidence on the involvement of Iraq and Afghanistan step-by-step becomes weak and weaker, we suggest that the war in Iraq and Afghanistan would be classified as a provoked war induced by a third party.

This would serve as a typical example that a third party can easily induce a war on an innocent country or a country whose behavior has been suspect for a long time or a country whose regime leads to unhappiness in other countries.

With respect to the current situation between China and Japan, what we mean by a third party induced war is that a third country, even a small group of people, can disguise their armed forces either as the Chinese armed forces to attack Japan or as the Japanese armed forces to attack China to provoke the third Sino-Japanese war.

Even the damage from an attack would not be as disastrous as the attack on the World Trade Center. Such an attack would provide a valuable opportunity and strong pretext for the warlike people in both China and Japan to ask their government to take a step towards the third Sino-Japanese war. However, if the damage of attack would really be as tragic as the attack on the World Trade Center, then no explanations and rationales would prevail over the sentiments that we need to severely punish the perpetrators and attack the country who host the perpetrators or the country who has been suspected to host the perpetrators.

Do we, the Chinese people and Japanese people, have no need to prevent such a stupid war provoked by a third party?

5.1 SUPER-NATIONALISTS

Can we not imagine that an armed force would pretend to be the Japanese air force and attack Chinese cargo ships? As there is no air defense system in any cargo ship, we would not expect to see any captive available to uncover the real perpetrators, China would certainly seek revenge for this attack. Similarly, a disguised attack can be easily made on Japanese cargo ships.

If history is correctly recorded, we can find many examples, where a country declared war on another country for the sake of a single important person or for some very trivial reason. When I say if history is correctly recorded, I mean, this type of war must have a deep profound reason rather than war for the sake of a single important person or some very trivial reason, which serves only as the pretext.

The war for the sake of a single important person in modern history appears less frequently than in early human history. However, we still can say that a single person could still provoke a war, for example World War I was provoked in such a way.

In our context, a single person could provoke the third Sino-Japanese war with the assassination of statesmen in either China or Japan. Of course, in such case we would expect to see the really extreme nationalist either in China or in Japan, such a person or a group of people do not need faked documents, they can conduct the assassinations for the sake of Chinese people or Japanese people. Let us assume that a Chinese student in Japan would try to assassinate the Japanese Emperor. What would the reaction be in Japan? Is this not a simple way to provoke a third Sino-Japanese war? If a super-nationalist would assassinate a statesman in either Japan or China; the retaliation would be extremely strong if a Chinese student in Japan would assassinate the Japanese Emperor. Again under the current poisoned atmosphere, it would not be difficult to find such a desperate "hero".

In practice, this type of assassination is not easily done, however can we not imagine a failed assassination under the faked name of a super-nationalist, but done by some groups of interest? Even, some shameful super-nationalists would claim responsibility for such an assassination although it may not be their plan or responsibility. This is not a fantasy but a probable case because currently less and less organizations dare claim their responsibility due to the fear of retaliation.

Of course, there are many ways to provoke a third Sino-Japanese war in the super-nationalists' mind and the mind of groups of special interests, for example, suicide bombers, hijacking of Chinese or Japanese airlines, cyber attacks, attacking economic centers, and so on, while we have no need to exhaust their ways over here.

5.2 UNNAMED COUNTRIES

Let us frankly face the following real, but bitter fact: both China and Japan are not popular if not hateful in East Asia and Southeast Asia regions for various reasons and rationales although both China and Japan pour money into these two regions to improve their images. Currently it would be easy to figure out why Japan is not popular in both regions because of the Japanese aggression during World War II, while it is not easy to figure out why China is not popular in both regions although to a lesser degree in East Asia region.

Could no country like to use such a possibility to let China and Japan down, to let them kill each other, to destroy their industries and countries? And then East Asia and Southeast Asia would become more "peaceful", less competitive, and less "threatening" from either China or Japan. Is this not a good opportunity? Is this not the best solution for East Asia and Southeast Asia?

In fact, a small-sized well-trained armed force could easily hijack both Chinese and Japanese governments into the third Sino-Japanese war. Let us assume that a small-sized, but well-trained armed force from Taiwan attacks both China and Japan simultaneously either near the disputed Diaoyu Islands or somewhere. This would certain bring the break of the diplomatic relationship between China and Japan, and then China and Japan would go along the pathway towards the third Sino-Japanese war.

5.3 MECHANISMS TO PREVENT PROVOKED WAR

Here, we should ask ourselves: Do we, the Chinese people and Japanese people, have any mechanism to distinguish a real super-nationalist from a fake super-nationalist? Do we, the Chinese people and Japanese people, have any mechanism to prevent the misinterpretation of any attack, which is similar to the attack to the World Trade Center, on Chinese soil and Japanese soil? Can we, the Chinese people and Japanese people, quietly and patiently listen to any accounts of the possible assassination of a Chinese statesman or Japanese Emperor? Actually, neither the Chinese government nor the Palace of the Japanese Emperor is guarded against such an unimaginable attack.

All this should be taken into account, because we have already witnessed the fact that Iraq deemed to be innocent from the attack on World Trade Center, but Iraq was invaded and Iraqi government was overthrown at least on the account that Iraqi government supported the attack on World Trade Center.

Take a step forward from here, we, all the people in the world, should ask whether the international organization or the international community has any mechanism to prevent such an unhappy event from occurring again.

It is doubtful that current international bodies would clarify any cloud over this type of incidence. This further indicates that the mechanism and structure of current international bodies are outdated.

If the international bodies cannot do anything to clarify these wrong doings and have no solution to the disastrous outcome, then we wonder whether the Chinese government or the Japanese government has any mechanism to prevent such a tragedy from happening.

Currently, it is highly likely that neither the Chinese government nor the Japanese government have any mechanism to prevent a third party induced war.

Therefore, we, both the Chinese people and Japanese people, should ask our governments whether they have any mechanism to prevent such a provoked war, and whether they plan to build such a mechanism, if they do not have any such a mechanism.

This demand is in great need because neither the Chinese government nor the Japanese government was designed to prevent the unheard of tragedy from falling upon us, upon the Chinese people and the Japanese people.

Communications at different levels between Chinese and Japanese governments need to be established. Mutual trusts should be built between China and Japan.

Chapter 6

CHINA'S PREPAREDNESS

There was a council of war held to consider what it was best to do. It was a council of perplexity and despair. Nobody could tell what it was best to do. To go back was disgrace. To go forward was destruction; and it was impossible for them to remain where they were.
— Jacob Abbott, Richard I [6]

Chinese history shows that China never seems to be fully prepared for war with a foreign country, no matter whether a foreign force invaded China or China planned to cross her border to fight in a foreign country. The cases where the Chinese armed forces fought beyond the Chinese borders were very rare.

No one previously answered the question of why China was so poorly prepared for a war with foreign forces, no one even attempted to analyze this inherited problem in detail. Perhaps, the unprepared China is always the case so we, the Chinese people, are already accustomed to this trend and do not feel anything strange.

If the unprepared wars are the trend in Chinese history, we would expect that China will once again not be prepared for the third Sino-Japanese war although many warlike people in China sing the songs that China will certainly defeat all the world powers.

To test China's preparedness, we would ask several simple questions. If we would have the answers, we would say that China has prepared for the third Sino-Japanese war, otherwise we would consider that China still goes along her historical trend that China is always unprepared for a war with foreign forces. Let us ask ourselves two simple questions:

Does China need a large-scale action in order to arm herself? Does China have the plans to change her industry into an arms race? Certainly and surely, we have no open answers.

6.1 WILL THE FUTURE BE DIFFERENT FROM THE PAST?

The first Sino-Japanese war resulted in the complete defeat of the Chinese government and humiliated treaty. The second Sino-Japanese war, although China claimed to be a winner, resulted in the casualties about 400,000 Japanese lives versus 20,000,000 Chinese lives. Clearly there are also various statistics on casualties related to China and Japan in the second Sino-Japanese war.

Anyway, the above either estimated or statistical casualties give a ratio of one versus fifty. Perhaps, this is the most costly war in human history, however we should realize that China had yet to defeat Japan with such a ratio of casualty during the second Sino-Japanese war if the western allies and the USSR did not defeat Japan. With this ratio of casualty, all the Chinese nationals would have been extinguished in the second Sino-Japanese war if Japan would have wanted to pay with ten million Japanese lives.

Honestly and frankly, but very much unfortunately, the Chinese films and literature describe the first and second Sino-Japanese wars in a very different way, that is, the cost-effectiveness seems to favor China rather than Japan, especially the second Sino-Japanese war, which seemed to have been an easy war for the Chinese armed forces.

These Chinese films and literature demonstrate how the war is very easy for Chinese armed forces, even for the ordinary Chinese people. We would say that these Chinese films and literature do not respect the history and are irresponsible. These films and literature ignored the great sacrifice of Chinese people and their pain and suffering.

Naturally, our question is whether the Chinese people still want to conduct a similarly costly third Sino-Japanese war? If the answer is no, then what should the Chinese people do to prevent another humiliation and unfair treaty?

In fact, the Chinese people never seriously asked themselves why China lost two wars with Japan. Although China claimed to be the winner of the second Sino-Japanese war, it was not the Chinese armed forces that made Japan surrender, but the American and Soviet forces. If no countries had supported China during the second Sino-Japanese war, Japan would not have hurt the interests of other world powers in China, and World War II would not have occurred, then the most likely scenario would be that the second Sino-Japanese war could have been prolonged for another 20 to 50 years. This is a very natural deduction from human trend, that is, no feudal country could defeat a capitalist country, which is why the UK can control such a large area around the world without much difficulties.

We, the Chinese people, need to find our weaknesses, but not boast how Chinese armed forces were great during the first and second Sino-Japanese wars.

In fact, the most crucial and serious question is how many lives the Chinese people are prepared to lose during the third Sino-Japanese war with the consideration of modern weapons of mass destruction.

6.2 PEOPLE'S PREPAREDNESS

Although there are many warlike-minded people and even super-nationalists in China, we should say that the Chinese people are unprepared. This is so because the historical trend in Chinese history clearly shows how easily foreign forces invaded China and controlled a large area inhabited with Chinese people without many difficulties.

The historical long-term peace makes the Chinese people totally underestimate the difficulty of any war with foreign forces. If we refer to the third Sino-Japanese war, then we would see that the Chinese people do not seriously consider all possible consequences of the third Sino-Japanese war.

The historical trend, particularly in reference to the first and second Sino-Japanese wars in the past and the third Sino-Japanese war in the future would be this. At the beginning, the Chinese people would have full confidence to defeat the foreign invaders as well as foreign forces. Many young Chinese ladies claim that they will certainly join the Chinese army to fight against foreign invaders, in this case, the Japanese armed forces. However the enthusiasm would soon exhaust, even die out if a major setback would be met. Then, the Chinese people would lose their confidence and hopes to defeat foreign invaders as well as foreign forces as the extremely difficult war goes on.

There are many factors in Chinese society as well as long-term trends in Chinese history, which would contribute to the difficulty in the involvement of the Chinese people in the third Sino-Japanese war. Let us now look at the possible and potential problems related to the preparedness of the Chinese people in current Chinese society.

The single-child policy would easily lead to each family to do their best to prevent their valuable and heavily invested child from joining the Chinese army, although initially this would not be the case because the Chinese films make the war as an excursion with beautiful girls, as a joyful game with pets, and as a fast track to become famous with more lovers, thus there would be more-than-needed young men who want to join the Chinese army. However, this would not be the case if the third Sino-Japanese war would continue for years or if the Japanese attacks would consume too many lives. The pain due to the casualty in the single-child family would spread across the nation after the initial casualties in the Chinese army, and each family would naturally do their best to bribe the corrupted officials to prevent their child from being enlisted. We can find many examples in Chinese history that rich people's sons had no need to join the Chinese army to defend China by bribing corrupted officials at various levels.

Actually, any political movement has a similar historical trend in China, for example, the political movement during the Chinese Cultural Revolution, the so-called up to the mountains and down to the villages movement, died very shortly after its launch although at the very early beginning many young men and women went to the countryside with great passion and enthusiasm [12].

The real question raised here is whether China can resist a psycho war due to the loss of a single child in a single-child family, which is certainly a disaster to the family.

On the other hand, human history shows that the so-called middle class is not a big fan in supporting their country to conduct any war, simply because the middle class would not risk their fortune to join any adventure as we read in Robinson Crusoe [13]:

> "mine was the middle state, or what might be called the upper station of low life, which he had found, by long experience, was the best state in the world, the most suited to human happiness, not exposed to the miseries and hardships, the labor and sufferings of the mechanic part of mankind, and not embarrassed with the pride, luxury, ambition, and envy of the upper part of mankind."

Many Chinese and foreign media advocate and applaud the rise of the middle class in Chinese society, so naturally the people from the middle class would not be likely to contribute much enthusiasm and energy into the enterprise of a third Sino-Japanese war.

Another fact taken into consideration is that the current and long-term trends in Chinese society are money-oriented, which once again cast shadow on the ability of China to endorse a war and whether the Chinese people can actively take part in the third Sino-Japanese war as we read in Monte Cristo [14]:

> "M. Danglars is a money-lover, and those who love money, you know, think too much of what they risk to be easily induced to fight a duel."

A big problem related to the third Sino-Japanese war would be whether the Chinese people would like to be evacuated to remote and rural areas when the rich and developed coast would be attacked by Japanese naval and air forces? More significantly, can Chinese people evacuate to remote and rural areas, and destroy their properties to prevent the Japanese army from advancing when the Japanese army lands in Mainland China. In the Chinese history, the Chinese people never destroyed their properties, their towns, their cities, and everything in their lands to prevent the invaders from advancing. This is indeed very different from European nationals as well as other nationals. For example, Russia used this strategy to prevent Bonaparte from advancing. We read the following as to how Saladin used this strategy to prevent Richard I from advancing [6]:

> "Destroying every thing, which could afford sustenance to William's army from the whole breadth of the land. To lay waste a country since a foreign army, just landed in the country, could not long remain inactive on the shore."

Actually, we can extend our view to super Chinese nationalists overseas, who no doubt love China, but can they risk being considered as Chinese spies to be jailed, and even lose their foreign citizenships during the third Sino-Japanese war, which is very like to lead to World War III?

6.3 CHINESE ARMED FORCES' PREPAREDNESS

Nowadays, China is already very different from the previously feudal China, which had little economic connection with the world. The industrialization in China leads the Chinese economy to become a part of the world economy. Now China and the Chinese economy heavily rely on imports and exports, because the overseas markets and raw materials are indispensable to the Chinese economy.

Thus, a serious question raised here is whether the Chinese navy force can secure the trade routes between China and the rest of the world? The same question would also be applied to Japan to a far less degree because the US navy can guarantee the safety of Japanese trade routes although Japan also heavily relies on imports and exports. Can China and Japan kill each other by sea blockade?

Can the Chinese navy win a battle of the Pacific, which could be equal to the Battle of the Atlantic? The first Battle of the Atlantic was limited to the Atlantic Ocean, North Sea, and Mediterranean Sea, and the scope of the second Battle of the Atlantic extended to the Atlantic Ocean, North Sea, Irish Sea, Labrador Sea, Gulf of St. Lawrence, Caribbean Sea, Gulf of Mexico, Outer Banks, and Arctic Ocean. If the third Sino-Japanese war would occur then followed by World War III, then the battles would extend to almost all the seas around the world. Does the

Chinese navy have the confidence to win this battle? The job for the Chinese navy is immensely huge because the battle will include at least both the Pacific Ocean and Indian Ocean.

Honestly our nationals, the Chinese nationals, are not the nationals who are most familiar with sea life. This is not because ancient China had no money to build the ships, but because the Chinese people had no such need in the past. Actually, many countries could offer a sizable naval force, but those countries had no such need, therefore they did not become a maritime country. China should be considered such a country, and confines herself in her territory, actually the region behind the Great Wall.

Here the question raised is why the Chinese people constructed the Great Wall along the north border rather than along the seacoast? The only answer was that the invaders were most likely to come from the north rather than from south along the Chinese seacoast. The implication is very clear: the Chinese people are the nationals who can engage a war only on land, but not on the sea. Of course, the time when the Great Wall was built was far beyond the development of navy in the world. Ironically, almost all the invaders since the 19th century arrived at China along the Chinese seacoast including the Japanese army. Clearly, the Chinese seacoast was the weakest part in all the Chinese defending lines. On the other hand, the Chinese seacoast contains the most advanced economic zones. Can the Chinese naval force protect and defend the valuable Chinese seacoast regions?

Now let us look at the Chinese air force. Can the Chinese air force prevent any bombardments from the Japanese air force? Can the Chinese air force defend Chinese global mega cities from Japanese attacks? Even US attacks? These are very serious questions presented before the Chinese air force, because any attack on the Chinese global mega cities would lead to unimaginable damage and loss of life. With the distance as short as between China and Japan, it is almost impossible to effectively and efficiently defend numerous highly populated Chinese mega cities. On the other hand, can the Chinese air force launch a pre-emptive attack on the Japanese air force facilities? Can the Chinese air force survive any pre-emptive attack on the Chinese air force facilities to launch the retaliations? Can the Chinese air force protect the Chinese airborne divisions landing in disputed islands as well as Japan? The reasonable answers to the above questions seem not to be very optimistic. Here, we can raise an example, the Chinese airborne division could not land in the area that suffered from the earthquake in 2008 due to poor weather, but had to walk into the epicenter.

Actually, many Chinese know about the war affairs related to the Chinese armed forces through Chinese films, and these films concentrate more on the wars on land. However, the third Sino-Japanese war would have extremely little business to do with any battle on land at least at the beginning stage. Actually, the situation would be very unhappy and unfortunate if the Chinese ground force would be heavily involved in the third Sino-Japanese war because this would implicitly suggest that the Japanese army would land on Chinese soil and fight in Chinese territory as the Chinese ground force would have a extremely small chance to fight in the Japanese soil. Nevertheless, the involvement of the Chinese ground force would again implicitly suggest huge suffering in ordinary Chinese lives because they might live in the area occupied by foreign forces.

6.4 ADMINISTRATIVE PREPAREDNESS

Honestly it seems that the Chinese administrative system is not prepared for the third Sino-Japanese war, because we have not yet seen any measures taken directed to the third Sino-Japanese war.

Objectively, the Chinese administrative system is very good at dealing with routine and ordinary issues, for example, attending meetings, presentations at various ceremonies, writing of reports. No doubt, this characteristic guarantees China to move smoothly towards the predefined goal. However, the Chinese administrative system is not designed to deal with incidences, which happen suddenly. Practically, the current Chinese administrative system is mainly designed for the economic development inside China since the beginning of Chinese reform, but totally not designed for the third Sino-Japanese war.

Therefore it would take years to transfer the Chinese administrative system to have double functions, economic development in peaceful time and multiple tasks in wartime.

Chapter 7

FROM PRETEXT TO WAR

The affairs of Corcyra and Potidaea, and the events that served as a pretext for the present war . . . This interval was spent in sending embassies to Athens charged with complaints, in order to obtain as good a pretext for war as possible, in the event of her paying no attention to them.
— Thucydides, The History of the Peloponnesian War [15]

No matter what the disputes and disagreements are between China and Japan, they would be considered to serve as pretexts. Then history might again follow such a pathway regarding the third Sino-Japanese war:

1) Pretext – indirect conflict – direct conflict – casualty – tolerable casualty – new pretext;
2) Pretext – indirect conflict – direct conflict – casualty – intolerable casualty – vengeance – attack – war.

Therefore, the question for us is not whether China or Japan would find a good pretext to initiate disputes and disagreements, but to find the casualty that either China or Japan feel intolerable, and cannot reconcile with each other. So we need at first to define what a casualty really means, i.e. the casualty could include loss of life, loss of money, loss of territory, loss of face, and so on and so forth.

Still, more importantly we should discuss the significance of casualty to the government rather than to the people because it is a government, which usually wages a war, rather than ordinary people, who have no power to declare any war.

7.1 TOLERABLE CASUALTY

Historically, the previous Chinese governments including ancient Chinese empires were indeed tolerant to the huge loss in territory, life, and money in order to reconcile with foreign invaders. Actually, we can find many such examples in Chinese history. Of course, the most recent example would be the second Sino-Japanese war, during which the Chinese government was unbelievably tolerant to such a huge casualty, i.e. the Japanese armies occupied almost all of northern China without major military action.

In this historical view, the Chinese government perhaps could be the most tolerant government in the world, because it could tolerate the loss of large territory, life and money in order to maintain a Chinese government in some remote places of China. As any Chinese government was composed of Chinese people, consequently we would say that the Chinese people perhaps are the most tolerant people in the world because the Chinese people could live under any governance no matter whether Chinese nationals or foreign nationals are governors. Take a step further; we would say that the Chinese thoughts are perhaps the most tolerant thoughts in the world because we, the Chinese people, do not care about many things beyond immediate personal need if we can survive.

Again, Chinese history clearly shows that the only standard of tolerance for most Chinese governments dated back from ancient Chinese empires was to maintain the stability of governments: if the foreign powers did not influence the life of Chinese empires or previous Chinese governments, then either Chinese empires or previous Chinese governments would be tolerant to the heavy loss in life, in territory and in money.

In this context, the current conflict between China and Japan appears to be tolerable because Japan does not demand a regime change in China, while the conflict between China and the US could become intolerable because many Americans advocate a regime change in China.

Clearly, the previous Japanese policymakers knew this peculiar Chinese characteristic; therefore the initial phase of second Sino-Japanese war appeared to be tolerable to the Chinese government.

The question is whether or not the current Japanese policymakers would use the same strategy to defeat China? Another way to state this question is whether Japan can become a Pacific Empire without hurting the Chinese government?

If this peculiar Chinese characteristic would still belong to the Chinese nationals, and if the trends in Chinese history would still prevail, then it would not be difficult for Japanese policymakers to find ways to take huge advantages from China within the limit of Chinese people's tolerance.

7.2 INTOLERABLE CASUALTY

Another principle for the so-called intolerable casualty for traditional Chinese thoughts would be that the foreign invaders should save the Chinese government's face rather than lose the Chinese government's face. To lose any Chinese government's face was generally intolerable, because it would endanger the existence of the Chinese government. Similarly, the humiliation to any Chinese government was generally intolerable because it would endanger the existence of the Chinese government.

Actually, the Chinese people loved their face value very much, and this peculiar Chinese characteristic could also be well known at least to our Chinese people. Thus, we can find that some Chinese empires even paid money to small surrounding kingdoms in order to trade for their recognition that they were subject to the Chinese empires. In reality, everyone knew very well that these small kingdoms were completely not subject to the Chinese empires, and totally independent of Chinese empires but were subsidized by Chinese empires. So we, the Chinese people, could spend money for an empty title to fill our pride.

This again follows our previous argument of whether the Japanese policymakers would wisely find a way that will not hurt Chinese pride and save the Chinese face to become a real Pacific Empire, for example, if China could pay the Japan a huge amount of money to silence the disputed pretexts such as territory, textbook, etc.

Nevertheless, our Chinese characteristic gives the world a chance to blackmail China.

If we look back the second Sino-Japanese war with the Chinese characteristic, then arguably Japan would have a larger chance to conquer China. This is so because Japan would have obtained much larger comprise and tolerance from the Chinese government if the Japanese policymakers did not want to overthrow the Chinese government, i.e. Nationalist (Kuomintang) government, but would have pretended or really wanted to help the Nationalist (Kuomintang) government to defeat the Communist Party of China.

Chapter 8

COLD WAR

It was one of those cases where, being obliged to go far, it is best to go
farther.
— Jacob Abbott, William the Conqueror [16]

Up until now, our analyses do not offer many options to reduce the tension
between Japan and China. Hence, it is very much likely that either China or Japan
would go along the traditional, even standard pathway that all the previous world
powers have undergone since the beginning of human history. Along this would-
be-power-has-to-go pathway, the first part of this road would be the so-called cold
war although this term was mainly related to the conflict in the 20th century.

To some degree, we should say that China has some experience on the cold
war. This is so because the cold war was mainly related to ideological differences.
In this regard, the cold war between China and the Soviet Union was through the
confrontations between Vietnam and Cambodia and between Albania and the
Soviet Union.

However this so-called cold war between China and Japan would not be
marked in such an ideological way, but would bear their particular characteristic.
This cold war between China and Japan would not reference to any ideological
difference, because both China and Japan are not exporters to export their
ideologies [5].

In fact, the equal power would be the base for conducting a cold war. In this
sense, we could actually say that the so-called cold war between China and Japan
has already begun since the time when China was somewhat equal to Japan at an
international stage, so either China or Japan began to find any pretext to accuse
the other country.

In some sense, the cold war works in legal frame, therefore all the options
seem to have to be selected in legal frame in order to avoid a direct confrontation.

8.1. COUNTRIES BENEFITED

As both China and Japan cannot export any of their original ideology to other countries, there would be fewer ideological followers in this so-called cold war between China and Japan. This furthermore means that this so-called cold war between China and Japan would mainly be related to these two countries.

Again since both China and Japan cannot export any of their original ideology, their life-style, their traditions, or their customs, both China and Japan could use only their money to buy the support from the rest of world. Thus this confrontation would create a valuable opportunity for many countries in the world to benefit from either China's or Japan's buy-heart investments.

The biggest benefited country in this case would be the US, because China would certainly pour money into the US in order to buy the Americans heart to give more support to China during the so-called cold war between China and Japan.

Actually, another big bloc of countries, which would benefit from the so-called cold war between China and Japan, would be the Southeast Asia countries, notably ASEAN. China and Japan are not very popular among these countries, which also do not play any leading roles in world affairs. However, China and Japan might secretly have the intention to build sea bases in ASEAN countries, which would serve the aim to create a Pacific Empire. This intention in both China and Japan would give the ASEAN countries the chance to draw investments, money, and political compensation from China and Japan.

Other potential countries, which will heavily benefit from the so-called cold war between China and Japan, would be European weaponry exporting countries, although there are various pretexts and obstacles for selling weapons to China. Therefore China would certainly lobby heavily in order to break an arms embargo because of the obstacles in European countries. In any case, the rearming of Japan and arming of China would be the greatest deal for arms industries either in the US or in Europe.

8.2. CHINESE WAYS IN COLD WAR

As there would not be many options on table to execute this cold war between China and Japan, we should pay attention to several Chinese options.

The first option that comes into Chinese people's mind would be the boycotting of Japanese products. Practically, that is the very traditional Chinese option that the Chinese people, mostly university students and intellectuals, advocate when the relationship between China and Japan or between China and any other country for example, the US, becomes worse.

This tradition, which might be dated back to more than one hundred years ago, is so long that no one really knows who was the first one to advocate the boycotting of Japanese products. Unfortunately, modern Chinese history did not credit this pioneer much because we have no evidence to demonstrate who was the inventor.

However, as a Chinese myself, I would say that the boycotting of Japanese products does not succeed at all, neither at national scale nor at local scale. It does not even work at all. The failure might be due to several factors: (i) the Chinese economy was far much more underdeveloped than the Japanese economy in the past. Therefore the so-called boycotting of Japanese products was actually the boycotting of new technology, the boycotting of new economic mechanisms and models, and the boycotting of social progress. It is indeed a laugh that a feudalism society with a few agricultural products could boycott a capitalism society with massive industrial products. (ii) Chinese and Japanese economies are very complementary nowadays, i.e. Japan mainly produces high quality and high tech products, while China produces mainly low-tech products, with sometimes very poor quality in Chinese markets. In such a case, it is also very difficult to boycott Japanese products.

Arguably, the call for boycotting Japanese products is in fact to sacrifice the Chinese people's interest by asking the Chinese people to buy the less competitive, lower quality but expensive Chinese products. This option could be considered unwise.

The second option that comes into Chinese people's mind would be to attack the Japanese people who are living inside China, to attack the Japanese embassy and consulates, and to attack foreign reporters. This is also a very traditional Chinese option as we could remember the attack on foreign reporters during Tiananmen Square Incident.

The Boxer Rebellion or the Boxer Uprising (November 1899 – September 1901), Yi He Tuan, in Chinese pronunciation, adopted this approach, which led to the intervention of the Eight-Nation Alliance and an extremely humiliating treaty.

Although this option is unwise, even unlawful, this option imposes a serious challenge not only to the Chinese government but also to the Chinese people, i.e. the Chinese government would be accused of "sale of country", mai guo, in Chinese pronunciation, if the Chinese government tries to stop such attacks.

The third option that the Chinese people used to do is to find various private scandals to mix with public affairs, with international relationships, and with disputes between countries. For example, during the demonstration against the bombing of the Chinese embassy in Yugoslavia, we could read such placards saying that Clinton was a big hooligan with reference to his relationship with Monica Lewinsky. Actually this option could not bring positive image on the demonstrators.

8.3. SPEED OF ARMS RACE

An important symbol of so-called cold war would be the arms race between China and Japan. An important question raised here is whether Japan would need to rearm herself? This question arises because Japan might need a decade, even a generation, to rearm herself with amending of the Japanese constitution. This approach would cost time, and money. Moreover this approach would raise alarm in the Asian countries previously occupied by Japan during World War II, and the suspicion from the US (see Section 3.3, Chapter 3).

Therefore, Japan might not need to rearm herself as preparing for the third Sino-Japanese war. This approach could be possible because Japan could borrow the US armed forces in the third Sino-Japanese war as the third Sino-Japanese war would certainly lead to the application of the security treaty between Japan and the US. In such a case, the speed of an arms race in the western Pacific Ocean and western part of Pacific Rim could reach to zero for Japan in comparison with Chinese military building up, which draws more and more suspicions and criticisms around the world.

Another possible outcome of an arms race would be the talks on arms control between China and Japan and between China and other countries when the speed of arms race reaches the maximum but without the hopes to win the arms race. In this context, the arms control talk would serve as a signal that the cold war approaches the end. However, we currently have yet to see the such a talk, thus we could judge that both China and Japan might still be at an early stage of the cold war, and there would be many years ahead before there could be a serious arms control talk between China and Japan, and between China and other countries.

8.4. HOSTAGES AND EXPELING

One of most common practices during the cold war is to expel spies from enemy country. No one recalled whether the previous Chinese dynasties and governments applied this common practice during their disputing era with foreign countries in the past.

Since the time that China opened, many Chinese people have been going abroad to pursue a better education and a better life, could Japan as well as other countries expel these Chinese people? Could the Chinese government take a counter-measure to expel the Japanese currently living in China?

Of course, the withdrawal of Japanese living in China as well as other nationals would be a clear message for ending the cold war. On the other hand, it would be unlikely that the Chinese government would recall her citizens from abroad.

In some dirty wars, the foreign nationals would be used as hostage and as human shield. Could we not imagine that the Chinese citizens would be put in cities as human shields to prevent the Chinese attacks? Similarly, could we not imagine that foreign citizens would be put in Chinese mega cities as human shields to prevent the foreign attacks?

8.5. FREEZING OF ASSETS

As the hostility increases, naturally the freezing of assets would appear above the horizon. Very likely, China would not have many ways to freeze the assets of Japan as well as the US, but China would be very much vulnerable to the prospective that the foreign governments would freeze the China's assets oversea.

At this stage, it is difficult to imagine the effect of freezing of assets on the Chinese economy as well as the Japanese economy. Also it is not clear whether the freezing of assets would affect the massive Chinese investments in the US as well as the Japanese investments in China.

Chapter 9

THE THIRD SINO-JAPANESE WAR

> There could be no peace between the rising civilization and the old, one of
> the two must destroy the other
> — Brooks Adams, The Theory of Social Revolutions [7]

If the cold war between China and Japan could not hurt each other much and international communities would still stay sidelined, then the hope for a peaceful solution to inhibit the ambition to become a Pacific Empire would sink beneath the horizon.

This would mean that all the politicians and technocrats either would have no ways to approach solving the problem or would have exhausted their options. If so, the military planners would take the leading roles in international affairs instead of politicians and technocrats. In such a case, we will really go towards the third Sino-Japanese war without any power to reverse this process.

9.1. DECLARED VERSUS UNDECLARED WAR

Since the end of World War II, the undeclared war has become fashionable and popular. Certainly, there must be many advantages to the country, which conducts a war without formal declaration. We might need to count these advantages with reference to both China and Japan to determine whether the third Sino-Japanese war would be an undeclared or declared war.

The history since World War II shows that the undeclared war seems to be a war between a militarily strong country and a militarily weak country. In this context, the declaration of war would not have any real meanings because it is the strong party decision as to whether the war would continue. Actually, the first phase of the second Sino-Japanese war was an undeclared war while both Japan and China were reluctant to declare war on each other. However, both China and Japan are somewhat equal nowadays therefore the third Sino-Japanese would become a declared war at a somewhat later stage after countless conflicts. On the other hand, the balance between China and Japan would become unbalanced if the US and NATO would immediately be involved in the third Sino-Japanese war, under such a circumstance the third Sino-Japanese war would be likely to be an undeclared war while the western allies could attack China as they like.

Actually, an undeclared war leaves much room for negotiation, which would be the biggest advantage for an undeclared war. In this context, both China and Japan would be very reluctant to declare a war on each other because both countries love their face value very much and each would try to find a way to negotiate if an initial conflict would result in no winner.

On one hand, the tough legislation could make the declaration of war difficult, on the other hand, many dictators might not need to pay any attention to the legislation mechanism therefore they might conduct any war they like. In this context, the declaration of the third Sino-Japanese war would become unlikely unless both countries suffer an intolerable casualty.

Still, an undeclared war could continue for many years with countless small, armed conflicts and countless talks between the two parties. Under current international fashion, this would be the best option before exhausting other options. In this sense, the declaration of war should be considered as the last option, very likely this is not the option either China or Japan would pursue. Therefore it is likely the first stage of the third Sino-Japanese war would be that each party wants to give the other party a lesson in order that the other party would not make more troubles and disputes.

In this manner, the third Sino-Japanese war would be the give-lesson war, which gives time for policymakers in both countries to consider what to do next, while the international bodies and would powers have sufficient time to decide their course. On the other hand, the declared war between equal powers would totally not be in policymakers' hand to control, because the declared war would go along its own particular way without paying any attention to politicians. The power to control a declared war would be in the hands of handful military officials, super military geniuses.

9.2. LIMITED VERSUS UNLIMITED WAR

History suggests that a limited war could reach a predefined goal only if a very strong country conducts a limited war with a very weak country. In such case, this limited war would generally be conducted on the soil of a weak country, while the strong country would still enjoy her normal life without any attack on her soil and with little worry of retaliation.

Following this rationale, the limited war would achieve little if nothing for countries with equal power. However, a limited war would be a test to find out the determination, resolution and patience of a hostile country. Chinese history shows that China generally could not pass the test of a limited war with foreign powers. Although there would be many reasons to account for this failure perhaps our Chinese philosophy would be the main underlined reason.

On the other hand, a limited war provides a base for negotiation, which could be a possible scenario for a limited third Sino-Japanese war, because the first Sino-Japanese war was in fact a limited war, while the second Sino-Japanese war could also be considered so before the occurrence of World War II. With strengthened muscle in Chinese military power, we would expect that a limited third Sino-Japanese war would be carried out in a very cautious way. However, we would not exclude the possibility that the limited third Sino-Japanese war would be carried out in a careless way because the Chinese armed force lacks experience in foreign war, in particular, war in the form of naval battles and air fighting. Still, we might need to ask whether a limited Sino-Japanese war would provide some material for bargaining between China and Japan in their future negotiation because talks seem unable to solve their disputes.

If we consider the boundary between limited and unlimited war between China and Japan, and between China and other countries, then we might assume that the attacks on popular cities in each country would lead to an unlimited war with the possibility of nuclear attacks. If so, the limited Sino-Japanese war would have limited options, for example, a sea blockade.

As both Japan and China are heavily dependent on oversea markets and resources, the sea blockade would be the first option for both China and Japan to conduct a limited third Sino-Japanese war. Thus, the question here is whether either China or Japan has enough warships to effectively and efficiently cut off other economic lines. Would this sea blockade impair other countries' interests? In fact, this sea blockade might not require bloodshed. Several pirate type warships in the open sea would be sufficient to threaten all the cargo ships to stay in port. Here, the question would be how much it would cost to use naval warships to escort cargo ships if we consider such a huge amount of cargo ships in operations.

The contemporary China is very different from the China during the first and second Sino-Japanese wars. China could survive quite well without any communication with the outside world because the Chinese economy was a self-sufficient feudal economy. Hence, the next question would be whether either China or Japan could survive the sea blockade long enough to let the other country kneel down to negotiations.

Following the sea blockade in a limited third Sino-Japanese war there would likely be the war on the disputed islands, notably Diaoyu Islands. Of course, the war on disputed islands would technically be related to the job of airborne force and marine as well as navy on the surface. However, the real question here is whether the capture and recapture of this island would be the beginning of the unlimited third Sino-Japanese war or the ending of the limited third Sino-Japanese war? This is a crucial problem for a limited war between somewhat equal powers because both parties would be likely to suffer similarly. Therefore, the war on the disputed island between China and Japan would totally be different from the war on the disputed island between the UK and Argentina in the so-called Falklands war in 1982, where the limited war was conducted between unequal powers.

In the limited third Sino-Japanese war, we would not expect to see the active involvement of Japanese allies, for example, the US, besides providing more modern weaponry to Japan. Economically, we should ask whether the world can stand the loss of Chinese markets and cheap products in a limited third Sino-Japanese war.

Of course, the cut-off value for our assumption related to the boundary between a limited and unlimited third Sino-Japanese war is that both China and Japan would not attack the intolerable targets in both countries, i.e. Mainland China and mainland Japan. If the limited third Sino-Japanese war would lose control and would become an unlimited war, then this unlimited third Sino-Japanese war would bring unimaginable damage to both the Chinese people and Japanese people. Much worse than that, this unlimited third Sino-Japanese war would certainly become World War III because the Japanese allies and the US allies including NATO would be involved. In other words, China would suffer attacks from almost all the world.

For the unlimited third Sino-Japanese war, we should ask at least two questions: (i) Who would survive? (ii) Should the foreign occupation need?

As there would be no borders, no front, and no home front in an unlimited war, a question for Chinese leaders and the Chinese people would be who should remain alive during an unlimited war between China and all Western allies? In particular, who would remain alive after nuclear attacks? This issue must be solved because any nuclear attacks on Chinese soil would easily result in an unimaginable loss in life and property.

Let us first look at this question before an unlimited third Sino-Japanese war occurs because we need the answer not only from the Chinese people but also from the policymakers in Western alliances.

For our Chinese people, if the nuclear attacks destroy the entire Chinese government, then who will lead the Chinese people to conduct the third Sino-Japanese war, even World War III? This means that the Chinese policymakers need to form a solid plan to decide who should survive after nuclear attacks. However, if the full protections would be given to the whole Chinese government and its administrative systems, then the young Chinese generation would suffer deadly nuclear attacks. Consequently China would have far less young workable men and women than China has today because China could be defined as an aging country. If the protection would list many rich people, then Chinese society would become unstable due to inequality.

For the western alliance, if the nuclear attacks destroy the entire Chinese government, then who would have the power to negotiate with the western allies? In many previous wars, the western alliance was used to set a new government composed of exiled political dissidents, who previously lived in western countries, however the question here is whether these inexperienced dissidents would be able to govern China? However, if the western allies would leave the whole Chinese government intact, then the war could continue for a quite long time and bear unimaginable loss.

Again, the next question for our Chinese people would be where would the people, who need to survive during nuclear attacks, hide in China? Any initiative along this line would lead to huge construction work, however if we, the Chinese people, would not build such a protective system then why we should be passionate about the war?

Can the Chinese land force occupy Japan? This is unimaginable, because the Chinese army historically has no experience on occupation in foreign land. Of course, one can become experienced through learning. On the other hand, do the policymakers in western allies plan to occupy China? Then, it would be an unbearable task to clean nuclear disasters in China, to feed the Chinese people, and so on until the Chineselization [5]. Then all their efforts would be in vain.

9.3 TRADITIONAL VERSUS SUPER-MODERN WAR

As China becomes strong and stronger, the Chinese people more and more talk about the renaissance of Chinese nationals. Therefore the Chinese traditions become more and more sunny, and the Chinese people become more and more convinced that they can use Chinese traditions to conquer the world.

With respect to the war, the Chinese people, as demonstrated by Chinese and Hong Kong films, very much like the hand-to-hand fighting with Chinese martial arts, which are valued as the Chinese treasure. Another tradition is the so-called Chinese spirit possession [16], which appears again and again in different historical periods of Chinese history, during which many Chinese people claimed that they were supernaturally invulnerable against any attacks no matter of whether the attack comes from gun or knife. Equipped with supernatural invulnerability, our previous generations of Chinese people tried in vain to defeat foreign invaders as we read [17]:

> "these Boxers were a very common lot, without education, and they imagined the few foreigners in China were the only ones on the earth and if they were killed it would be the end of them. They forgot how very strong these foreign countries are, and that if the foreigners in China were all killed, thousands would come to avenge their death. Yung Lu assured me that one foreign soldier could kill one hundred Boxers without the slightest trouble"

Actually, the war in most Chinese minds is a traditional war, fighting within a very short distance. Many Chinese people still have the concept obtained from some Chinese films to consider that the use of a warship to collide with an enemy warship is a way to conduct a battle on the sea.

However, modern Chinese history already shows that China could not win any war against foreign invaders using her proudly traditional war. More ironically, China even did not win many traditional wars in her history before gunpowder was invented.

Of course, the traditional war we discussed above is still related to what is in the Chinese mind. Militarily and historically, the traditional Chinese war was usually the wars on Chinese soil, which meant great suffering to the ordinary Chinese people, the loss of huge territory, reduction of government income, and so on and so forth.

Would we, the Chinese people, still prefer this type of traditional war? Actually the traditional Chinese war was a war that a weaker party had to conduct in such a pitiful way against the stronger party. This traditional Chinese war is a sign of weakness and powerlessness.

Certainly, the third Sino-Japanese war would be a modern war, not only because the Japanese armed forces defeated the Chinese armed forces during the first and second Sino-Japanese wars by conducting a modern war, but also more importantly the modern war, super modern war, would be the only way to defeat China.

At this point, we, the Chinese people, must admit that the Chinese armed forces significantly lack experience on modern wars than European and world powers. As we wrote in the previous chapter (Section 2.9, Chapter 2), the US troops are the most experienced troops in modern warfare. This simply means that we would not expect to see a Chinese victory at the beginning of the third Sino-Japanese war. This is so because Roosevelt suggested that the army trained in peaceful time is useless [18].

9.4 SHORT-TERM VERSUS LONG-TERM WAR

Without involvement of the US and NATO, the strength between China and Japan would be somewhat equal. Under the condition that no US and NATO troops would be involved in the third Sino-Japanese war, this war would be a limited war. As a limited war between equal powers could not settle and seal any disputes, this limited war would be a chronic disease, which would take years after years without any solution.

This is not unimaginable, as we have seen that the separation between the two Koreas has already been longer than six decades, the separation between China and Taiwan has already been longer than six decades, and the armed conflicts between Israel and Palestine has already been more than six decades.

A long-term third Sino-Japanese war would provide the best opportunity for world arms industries with consistent orders from both China and Japan. On the other hand, a long-term third Sino-Japanese war would have very negative effects on valuable Chinese mega cities along Chinese seacoast, simply because the people might abandon those mega cities due to the fear of attacks. If this would occur, the consequence for the Chinese economy would be profound because these Chinese global mega cities are the powerhouse of the Chinese economy.

In some sense, the long-term third Sino-Japanese war would be different from the current situation between two Koreas and between China and Taiwan, since both Koreas, and both China and Taiwan, do not have endless armed conflicts.

Therefore, the question raised here is whether the international community could help to establish the demilitarized zone between China and Japan although the countries have no common borders. Perhaps the demilitarized zone would be the solution for a long-term third Sino-Japanese war, and would avoid negative impact on the world economy.

Chapter 10

JAPAN'S ALLIES

Nations have no permanent friends or allies, they only have permanent interests.
—Lord Palmerston [19]

Japan in fact has chained allies, the first direct and immediate ally is the US. Through the US, Japan can get military support from almost all the western countries, at first place, NATO. So if the US would actively take part in the third Sino-Japanese war, then Japan would get support from almost every corner of this globe. This is so simply because the US has so many treaties signed with each and every country around the world.

Perhaps, this is the best way to maintain peace because uncountable nations guarantee the sovereignty of a single country. Very likely, there were no such complicated chained allies before World War II, thus the chained allies would be considered as an invention to guarantee a country's sovereignty.

If we would consider Japan's allies, the third Sino-Japanese war would be equal to the war with all western allies, then with almost all the allied countries in the world. Thus, the third Sino-Japanese war would be unique in world history, even in human history, because no country dares wage a war against the whole western alliance or alliance from most parts of the world. If China would wage a war against Japan, it would be an unprecedented event, i.e. to use a single country's force to wage a war against the western world.

The former Soviet Union with her strong alliances did not dare to engage a war against any country in the western alliance, while the US did not dare to wage a war against any country in the eastern alliance although both the USSR and the US tried to defeat others through the war in the third world.

China is not a representative of any political, military, even economic bloc (see Chapter 11), therefore China has almost no chance to wage a war against

Japanese interests through a third country as the US and USSR did in almost the second half of the 20th century. Although Japan belongs to a political, military and economic bloc led by the US, Japan like China has no way to engage a war against Chinese interests through a third country. Therefore any disputes and disagreements between China and Japan can in principle only be solved through a direct confrontation between China and Japan rather than through a third country.

Accordingly, we should analyze and define the boundary, beyond which the direct confrontation between China and Japan would go along an irreversible pathway towards the third Sino-Japanese war leading to intervention from the US, and then from NATO. On the other hand, if both China and Japan do not pass this predefined boundary, then any disputes and disagreements between China and Japan could be considered as the show, which politicians and super-nationalists play for votes and fun.

Another question to be answered is whether the western alliance led by the US would adopt the policy used by the UK and France during the beginning of World War II, as we know, when the UK and France guaranteed the safety of Poland but really did little in this regard. Can we not imagine that the US and her western alliance would not do so again?

Actually, we could consider that China and Japan have entered the cold war, because the disputes and disagreements between China and Japan have already upgraded to the disputes and disagreements on territory. This is the most famous or notorious pretext for any war between two countries in human history.

If the disagreements between China and Japan would be only focused on the disputed islands, one might suggest a solution that would make these disputed islands completely disappear as we have seen the case of Bermaja in Gulf of Mexico [20]. However, even if the disputed islands between China and Japan would disappear, both countries would soon find a new pretext to raise the tension between them.

During the cold war between China and Japan, the US and her western alliance had little to do simply because there is always some territorial dispute in the world, and actually no one knows how to solve these territorial disputes for good because these territorial disputes arise anyway.

If the US would return to her famous isolationism, which the US applied for a quite long time, the boundary for US involvement would be somewhat clear, i.e. the US would not be involved in any war if the war would hurt for American lives. Actually, there would still be the possibility of reemerging isolationism in the US along with decaying of the US role in world affairs if we project the third Sino-Japanese war to take place from now to fifty or one hundred years. Still, if we project the third Sino-Japanese war from now to fifty or one hundred years,

Japanese interests might change during this period of time. For example, Japan might become more ambitious, which would lead to a conflict with the US. In such a case, the US would possibly be China's ally as we have seen what happened during World War II.

Without the full involvement of the US, Japan would have relatively few reliable allies in the western Pacific Ocean as well as western part of Pacific Rim. The question raised here is whether China would be able to cut off Japan's chained allies in order to prevent a "chain reaction" to the third Sino-Japanese war. The possible answer is very likely to be No, because these chained allies are based on a similar ideological concept, similar social mechanism, and somewhat similar interests. In this argument, we would suggest that Japan would be the representative of these blocs in East Asia.

This means that Japan would still hold a solid position in these blocs if Japan would not change her social mechanism and ideological concept. Historically, Japan is a country more resistant to foreign ideologies than China therefore Japan would have a smaller chance than China to follow any fashionable ideology popular in the world regarding the radical changes in social mechanism. Therefore there would be a far smaller chance that Japan would depart from her current allies, especially with the increased tension between China and Japan.

Chapter 11

CHINA'S ALLIES

One should care to sweep the snow in front of his own door, but not care the
frost on the roof of other's house (Implication: One should care his own affair but
not other's affair).
— A Chinese proverb

Traditionally and historically, China is not a country allied with other
countries, because the geographical location of China was somewhat isolated and
the Chinese people's narrow interests were totally confined within Chinese
territory.

At some historical moments, i.e. the Chinese dynasty was somewhat stronger
compared with the immediately previous Chinese dynasty. The Chinese
government could ally with one or several very small countries with the real aim
to show that China was great and strong. Of course, the pre-condition for such an
alliance was that these small countries should officially acknowledge that China
was their superior and they were subject to Chinese governance on the surface
although China might pay money for this recognition. Actually this type of
alliance was an alliance for Chinese face value and self-contentment rather than
for mutual development and defense.

Generally speaking, China had no allies in any potentially armed conflicts
during Chinese history, if we distinguish armed conflict different from a declared
war.

The first Sino-Japanese war seemed due to the fact that the Chinese
government would like to honor her duty or treaty upon request from the Korean
government.

After the creation of the Peoples Republic of China, China seemed to have a
good treaty with the former Soviet Union, which could in principle be an ally if
China would be involved in any open war. However, this treaty had reached its

end without extending it due to the differences between China and the USSR. Since then, China seemed to have no intention to ally with any country in the world.

11.1 IS CHINA A REPRESENTATIVE OF ANY BLOC?

As Chinese history clearly and evidently shows that China has few allies, there must be some profound reasons of why China could not form any reliable alliance. Naturally, the traditional Chinese philosophy, which suggests that a Chinaman should not care for other peoples business and others should not care for mine, could have been applied to the relationship between countries.

Another interesting observation on Chinese history suggests that the Chinese people in fact do not have any interest in any alliance. However, this observation does not mean that the Chinese people are too selfish. Logically, this observation seems to contradict the fact that Chinese philosophy pays much attention to the so-called relationship, mostly inter-personal relationship. In reality, the Chinese people generally apply this inter-personal relationship to the international relationship and the relationship between countries.

In particular, the Chinese international relationship is more or less related to the so-called friendship between peoples living in two countries. Under this concept, the Chinese people very much like to spend money to buy people's hearts in order to develop the so-called friendship.

This could be arguably the old-styled or Chinese styled diplomacy. This is so because the current international relationship is not based on so-called friendship between peoples living in different countries, but is mainly based on mutual interests either in economic development or in ideological concepts or in religious concepts or in social systems, and so on and so forth. This suggests that the old-styled or Chinese styled diplomacy could have difficulty forming any alliance with other countries.

Actually, China does not represent any political bloc, ideological bloc, economic bloc, religious bloc, or military bloc in any part of the world although the Chinese people have poured in a huge amount of money, for example the Olympic games in Beijing in 2008, to buy people's hearts to develop the so-called people's friendship.

We would argue if China could not serve as representative for any bloc, we would not expect to see China having the possibility to have any reliable alliance.

11.2 POLITICAL ALLIES

Since the creation of the People's Republic of China, China's allies have generally been political allies based on the same or similar ideological concepts. Through the history of the People's Republic of China, we can see changes in ideologies, which lead China to have different allies during different periods of time.

At the early stage, China's political allies mainly included the former Soviet Union and her satellite states, as well as newly independent countries. This political alliance was based on the concept of socialism, Marxism, and Leninism. This political alliance, though short-lived, provided a potential base for military alliance because communism advocates a socialist country to help other socialist countries in every way. The strong involvement of the Soviet Union in Asia, Africa and Latin America is evidence that a political alliance would turn into a military alliance. The Korean War could also serve as an example that a political alliance could turn out to be a military alliance.

Since worsening of the relationship between the USSR and China, China began to advocate the so-called Non-Aligned Movement, thus China has no more political allies in this regard because the Non-Aligned Movement included countries with different political backgrounds. However, the common concept for this Non-Aligned Movement was that no foreign country could interfere with another country's affairs, especially internal affairs. Although this type of alliance could draw attention from many countries, it appears attractive mainly during peaceful times because any war needs help from real allies.

During the Cultural Revolution, the only political ally for China was Albania. Actually, this alliance was not based on any similarity of ideological concept, but was based on the similar fate. Both China and Albania left the Soviet Union bloc because of their differences in ideology. However, the real fact is that both China and Albania were the countries with underdeveloped economies but strong feudal characteristics, so their departure would be attributed to their mindset of feudalism, which is different from the mindset of socialism. Actually, this alliance would do nothing during a war related to each of these two countries.

During the late stage of the Cultural Revolution, a political ally for China was the Khmer Rouge. Actually, this ally was generated from China's displeasure and dislike of the close relationship between Soviet Union and Vietnam. It was not clear whether China had any military agreement with Khmer Rouge, however this alliance ended up with nothing achieved.

At a much later stage of the Cultural Revolution, China was interested in a somewhat political alliance that was the third world. However, the third world was not defined according to any ideological concept, but rather an economic status. This bloc represented the countries with underdeveloped economies.

Since the reform took place in China, it is really hard to find whether China has any political ally, because the ideological concept becomes more and more obscure in modern China. Actually, this is the real long-term trend for the Chinese people in Chinese history, because the Chinese people generated fewer, if any, ideological concepts related to fair distribution of social wealth and execution of social justice [5]. Thus, it is very difficult for China to form an international political alliance based on ideology.

Logically, China could have taken responsibility for a socialist bloc, since China is a socialist country, after the collapse of the Soviet Union and her bloc. Accordingly, China could have become the leader of the socialist countries bloc including North Korea, Vietnam, Cuba, Yugoslavia, Syria, and perhaps several other countries. But practically, China has no interests in these socialist countries at all because the Chinese people feel these socialist countries are poor under the popular concept, which has prevailed over the last 20 to 30 years.

On the other hand, China does not agree with the concept that China is a capitalist country, thus China cannot join any political alliance based on political or ideological concepts.

Historically, China has no tradition to grant asylums on the basis of political and ideological differences. In this way, it is hard for China to find political supporters around the world.

Without political allies, the Chinese government would have great difficulty in calling the ceasefire at the UN if an armed conflict occurs or an open war is declared. The Chinese government would have great difficulty passing any meaningful resolution in any international organizations to defer any Japanese measures. For example, the WTO could rule out that China violates the WTO treaty to boycott any Japanese products.

11.3 MILITARY ALLIES

To the best of my knowledge, China has the tradition of forming small-sized military alliances with one or two small countries exclusively around China. In such an alliance, China played a role protecting these small countries on the surface, and this superficial role was well suited to the arrogant feelings of the Chinese.

However, China seems to have no real interests at all in building a military alliance with her neighboring small countries simply because such a thought is currently beyond Chinese consideration.

Militarily and strategically, no military alliance with surrounding countries along the Chinese border suggests that there is no buffer zone between China and other regional powers and world powers. Practically, this would lead to zero time for China to execute her reaction, and leave no room to negotiate any truce between China and other regional powers as well as world powers. In case the tension between China and other regional powers as well as world powers increases progressively, the Chinese army may have to assign significant manpower, weaponry as well as logistic facilities to safeguard Chinese borders because the surrounding countries are not China's military allies.

11.4 UNRELIABLE ALLIES

Honestly and frankly, China is not a reliable ally historically. For example, China might have promised the Khmer Rouge something with respect to the possible Vietnamese invasion although there were no unclassified documents to support this argument. However, history shows that many Chinese high-ranked officials visited Cambodia before the Vietnamese invasion, which certainly encouraged the Khmer Rouge to take a strong and provoking position against Vietnam and even gave some illusion that China would guarantee the safety of Cambodia.

After the Vietnamese invasion, there was a small-scaled armed conflict between China and Vietnam along their border. However, the Vietnamese army did not withdraw from Cambodia after the armed conflict between China and Vietnam. Thus, the alliance of the Khmer Rouge with China did not guarantee the territorial integrity of Cambodia and the power of Khmer Rouge.

Of course, nowadays the Chinese people do not know much about the Khmer Rouge. Many intellectuals would like to look at the cruelty of the Khmer Rouge rather than looking at whether or not the Chinese Communist Party or Chinese government could have had any treaty with Khmer Rouge to guarantee the safety of Cambodia.

Theoretically and logically, the Khmer Rouge would not dare take so strong a position against Vietnam without Chinese support. At that time, the Chinese policy disliked Vietnam because the Chinese leaders considered Vietnam an ally of the USSR, which was China's ideological enemy. Even without any secret treaty between the Chinese government and Khmer Rouge, the Chinese leaders, at least, put their dislike into the minds of Khmer Rouge leaders.

Another contemporary but trivial story would be that China behaved to support Yugoslavia during the US and NATO bombing campaign against Yugoslavia not only because of the bombardment on the Chinese embassy in Belgrade but also because Yugoslavia was a likely socialist country. However China easily abandoned her position to support Yugoslavia very soon after ending the bombing campaign, and rejected the asylum of Yugoslavia officials.

As a permanent member in the UN Security Council, China rarely uses her veto power in any international issue. Also China rarely expresses her view on any international affairs under the policy of not intervening in internal affairs of other nations. In return, we would expect to see that China would get little support from other countries when China needs to pass a political resolution to defend her own interest in the event of armed conflicts.

11.5 WHO CAN BE CHINA'S ALLY?

Under current discussion, China would have great difficulty forming any political alliance because China is not a representative of any ideological concepts besides the thoughts of ancient Chinese sages.

Arguably, the only possible ally who has the potential to help China in a third Sino-Japanese war in this region would be Russia, but there is no common language between China and Russia regarding ideological concept. It is even difficult to define Japan as the common enemy of China and Russia.

To some degree, the Chinese people seem to prefer the strategy "Befriend a distant state while attacking a neighbor" [21], which was once advocated and applied by an ancient Chinese military talent, Fan Sui, to conquer several states during the Warring States Period [22]. This Chinese strategy has such a profound influence that we can find its influence in Chinese foreign affairs; for example, China has problems with almost all her neighboring countries. Arguably, this strategy could be applicable when China's neighboring countries are weaker than China and China has the ambition to conquer these countries, however the real situation since the beginning of the 19th century has been that there are two powerful nations, Russia and Japan, who are China's neighbors, and most of time Russia and Japan were stronger than China either in military sense or in economic sense.

Chapter 12

INTERNATIONAL AND NEIGHBORING COUNTRIES' POSITIONS DURING THE WAR

Princes do keep due sentinel, that none of their neighbors do ever grow so (by increase of territory, by embracing of trade, by approaches, or the like), as they become more able to annoy them, than they were.
—Francis Bacon, Of Empire -- The Essays of Francis Bacon [1]

During the cold war between China and Japan, the international community and neighboring countries indeed have not much to say and do, simply because the disputes and disagreements between China and Japan are mainly related to these countries, their interests and their ambitions in East Asia, the western Pacific Ocean, and the western part of the Pacific Rim. In fact, many countries want no business with these trivial disputes and disagreements such as modification of school textbooks and visiting of shrines.

However, this would not be the case if the third Sino-Japanese war would occur, because this war would be considered a pretext and prelude towards World War III due to the chained security treaty through the US to many countries in the world. Thus, we have a picture of the world during the third Sino-Japanese war.

12.1 OIL EXPORT COUNTRIES

A currently silent, but very powerful force would be the countries selling their crude oil to China. This force in fact would have much to say either during the cold war between China and Japan or during the third Sino-Japanese war. Actually, this silent force could also have something to say to Japan, however this effect would be smaller than the effect on China. This is so because the US navy as well as the NATO navy would secure the safety of transport of oil from this currently silent force, to Japan.

On the other hand, if the OPEC (Organization of Petroleum Exporting Countries) would not exist when the third Sino-Japanese war occurs, then the decisive force would be the country, which sells crude oil for China and Japan. This naturally leads to the question of whether China needs to change her oil import strategy from the Middle East and Africa to nearby countries, such as Russia as well as Central Asia countries. Another uncertain factor would be whether the US would once again be a big exporter when oil in other countries is exhausted.

Scientifically, the oil expert countries would have not much to say if the new generation of weapons would not require much oil. However, it is not clear whether resource-economic weaponry systems are on the agenda of arms industries.

It is a pity that OPEC did not have a permanent member representative in the UN Security Council. Otherwise, OPEC would have a more decisive role in world affairs.

12.2 TAIWAN'S POSITION

The very basic concept that we should bear in mind would be that Taiwan has been separated from Mainland China for more than six decades, thus the gravity would become less and less after such a long separation.

Therefore, Taiwan's position would be very strange and peculiar during any armed conflict or open war between China and Japan.

This is so not just because Taiwan has a small army, which might not play any significant role in any directly armed conflict between China and Japan, but because Taiwan has a military treaty with the US, which guarantees Taiwan's security.

The question here is whether Taiwan would fight the Japanese army along with the troops from Mainland China under the condition that the Japanese army would not attack Taiwan first. If this would be case, the attack from Taiwan would invoke the treaty between Japan and US, which guarantees Japan's safety. By contrast, the attack on Taiwan by Japanese troops would invoke the treaty between Taiwan and the US. In either of both cases, it is highly likely the US treaty with Taiwan would weigh far less than the US treaty with Japan, then the natural result of the treaty between the US and Taiwan would be null.

This possibility would clearly be in the Taiwanese mind, thus Taiwanese troops would be very unlikely to be involved in any conflict between Mainland China and Japan although Taiwan consistently claims the sovereignty of Diaoyu Islands.

The above discussion on Taiwan's position is in fact quite positive, which is based on the assumption that the Taiwanese people have the same feelings as the Chinese people towards Japan. On this assumption, the most likely outcome from Taiwanese government would be neutral. Now let us see Taiwan's position from a negative view, which should be taken into consideration.

If Chiang Kai-shek were still alive, then Taiwan would use the opportunity of the third Sino-Japanese war to attack Mainland China to restore their power with the help of Japanese, US and NATO troops.

However, Chiang Kai-shek died long ago together with his will. Thus the third Sino-Japanese war would provide the best opportunity for the Taiwanese to declare their independence from Mainland China. Unfortunately, China has no way to prevent this independence in such a case because China would be fully involved in the third Sino-Japanese war.

12.3 SOUTH KOREA'S POSITION

In previous Sino-Japanese wars, Korea served as a passage for the Japanese army to pass through. If both Chinese and Japanese armies could meet on land, then the only way for the large-scale landing of Japanese armies would be South Korea. In an extremely unlikely and impossible case, South Korea would serve as the place the Chinese armies would go to land in Japan.

Thus, South Korea's position is extremely important. In principle, South Korea has the security treaty with the US, and the American troops station in South Korea. In this view, the government in South Korea could allow the passage of the Japanese army. However, the free and safe passage of South Korea should be under the condition that North Korea should be totally defeated and disarmed by Japan, South Korea and the US.

The real question is whether the Korean people would allow the passage of the Japanese army through their country to fight China as [23]:

"An army is always a burden and a curse to any country that it enters, even when its only object is to pass peacefully through."

Thus, an undetermined factor would be how long Japan and the US would take to disarm North Korea without intervention from China and Russia. This is the precondition for the safe passage of the Japanese army into China.

In fact, South Korea's view might not weigh much in the US and Japan's mind although the Chinese people pay much respect to South Korea because history indicates that Japan did not spend much effort conquering all of Korea. The real question is whether South Korea would be put into the bosom of North Korea in a desperate situation with the hope that the nuclear arsenals in North Korea would defend her independence? In such a case, the united Korea would become an important buffer to separate either China or Japan from a large-scale landing operation.

12.4 NORTH KOREA'S POSITION

It is very certain that North Korea will be in a close line with China in either the third Sino-Japanese war or any war between China and Japan's western allies. From this viewpoint, it seems that there would be little reason to discuss North Korea's position.

However, what really needs to be discussed is whether the pro-China North Korea government can stay in power during the third Sino-Japanese war? Can we not assume that some force would overthrow the North Korea government before the third Sino-Japanese war? In that case, we would very sadly see that all the countries surrounding China would have a somewhat hostile attitude towards China.

From this strategic view, it is the duty of the Chinese government and Chinese people to prevent the North Korean government from sliding into the alliance, which holds a hostile attitude to China although many modern Chinese have no interests in North Korea because they feel North Korea is poor.

An important question raised here is whether a nuclear-armed North Korea is more stable or is a disarmed North Korea more stable? Of course, this question is a big topic, which needs to be addressed in other places. Still, we should ask whether a united Korea would threaten the world.

If we project the time of the third Sino-Japanese war to be from now to fifty or one hundred years in the future, then one might really wonder whether both Koreas would still have common interests to unite after being separated for so long and if the difference between them would be so sharp.

12.5 INDIA'S POSITION

Since the middle of the 20th century, China and India became rivals in almost every way, the dispute about Chinese and Indian borders have yet to be settled. And the war between China and India in the 1960s cast a shadow on the improvement of relations between two countries. Therefore, India's position is extremely important.

More importantly India is a nuclear capable country, although the people in the world are not accustomed to see this fact. However, every rationale tells us that we should treat India differently with respect to her potential military and economic power.

If the third Sino-Japanese war would be a small-scale war, then we would expect to see India take a somewhat neutral position, or a somewhat hostile position. In both cases China would have to station a large army in both Tibet and Tibetan regions.

If the third Sino-Japanese war would be a full-scale war, then China would be in a very unfavorable position. India could use her nuclear weapons to pressure China to solve the unsolved disputed border problems forever. This is so because (i) China might have no more nuclear weapons in hand after attacks and counter-attacks using nuclear weapons, and (ii) China might need to free a large amount of armies stationed in Tibet and Tibetan regions to relocate somewhere else. In these circumstances, China's position would be much weaker than India's because India would still have sufficient nuclear weapons and intact troops to use.

Actually, the world would soon be accustomed to the use of nuclear weapons if a dozen nuclear weapons were used in the third Sino-Japanese war, or in World War III. If this is the case, then India might use her nuclear weapons to blackmail China.

Therefore, China should consider whether it would need a non-aggression pact with India.

12.6 RUSSIA'S POSITION

Russia's position would be particularly important during the third Sino-Japanese war not only because Russia might become the most important oil and gas supplier for China but also Russian ambition might once again become too strong to be accommodated within her current territory. This would suggest that

Russia, with her military might and natural resources, would re-dominate Central Asia.

If this would be the case, China might need to give up a part of her territory to exchange for support from Russia either in natural resources or in military equipment. It is not clear whether there would be such a bargain because Chinese history suggests that China sometimes used her land to trade for peace.

As Russia could be the only powerful ally with China, one might need to consider whether China needs a new non-aggression pact with Russia.

Strategically, Russia might not need to be involved in the war in the western Pacific Ocean or the western part of the Pacific Rim, but wait for the chance to restore and expend her influence, even territory, in Europe when all of NATO would enter the third Sino-Japanese war in the Pacific Ocean.

12.7 MYANMAR'S POSITION

If ocean oil imports would be completely or partially cut off by the Japanese blockade, then Myanmar would play a vital role in the Chinese economy. However, how the oil could be transported to Chinese economic and political centers would be a question, because the southwestern region in China is underdeveloped compared with other regions in China.

In every sense, Myanmar would take a neutral position during the third Sino-Japanese war. This suggests that China might need to reconsider her focus in development and move to remote areas of China but closer to oil resources.

Chapter 13

DISENGAGEMENT FROM WAR

If we can win, then we fight; if we cannot win, then we run away.
— Mao Zedong

The painful experience in human history on war is that it is very hard and difficult for a country, which actively wages an ongoing war, to disengage from the war. Perhaps, this is the most painful lesson in war history. For a recent example, there is almost no way for the US and her allies to disengage from the war in Afghanistan without losing face. In this context, actually, losing face for the US and NATO is a relatively trivial issue in this modern war, because the disengagement does not guarantee the safety of US and NATO countries free from any potential attack from Afghanistan soil, nor guarantees the safety of US and NATO countries free from any potential attack on their own soil.

Nowadays, the strong country's strategy, a decisively and rapid pre-emptive attack with fast disengagement, could not prevent any retaliation from a weak country.

The question is whether China, Japan, the US, and NATO countries would have a decent and face-saving way to disengage from the third Sino-Japanese war without signing unfavorable treaties?

13.1 CHINESE WAY TO DISENGAGE FROM WAR

In general cases, the honorable disengagement from a war is only possible for the winning party, and almost impossible for the losing party without losing land and heavy reparation. Historically it is rare that the winning party would allow the disengagement of the losing party from an open war, but the winning party would certainly and decisively defeat the losing party completely.

If we, the Chinese people, look at Chinese history, we would not feel cheerful and comfortable because the previous Chinese governments and armed forces had almost no way to disengage from a war with foreign forces without humiliating treaties. This simply means that China was a loser, and was forced to disengage from a war.

Thus, the third Sino-Japanese war would definitely be related to the fate of the Chinese people as a nation, and be related to the fate of China as an independent country. This is so because China is very much unlikely to win a war against Japan with her allies ranging from the US to each member of NATO, to almost all the western allies.

Therefore we should ask whether there are face-saving ways for China to disengage from the third Sino-Japanese war. This question seems to never come into Chinese minds.

In general, China's ways to disengage from a war would be classified as two types according to Chinese history.

If the enemy was stronger than China, China had no way to disengage from the war. The war would be conducted as the Israeli-Palestinian conflict, where Israel had the possibility to be either engaged or disengaged as a strong party in an armed conflict. In front of strong invaders, the feudal Chinese governments had only one choice, to retreat from the Chinese border to inland China and to make a series of peace deals to maintain the existence of feudal governments.

If the enemy was weaker than China, the Chinese people would tease the enemy to show how great we, the Chinese people, were. This certainly is our Chinese tradition, i.e. we prefer war with foreign nationals as described in the classic Chinese novel, Three Kingdoms or Romance of Three Kingdoms, from chapter 87 to chapter 90 [24], in which there was a war between Han national and ethnic minorities. In this war, the Chinese representative, Han national, captured the head of rebellions seven times until those rebelled people were fully convinced that they could not do anything against Han national, then the Han armies withdrew without leaving any Han national. This is the way that the Chinese people prefer to disengage from a war.

The most recent wars or regional conflicts with India (Sino-Indian war, 1962) and Vietnam indicated that the Chinese army would rapidly withdraw from occupied lands. They left all the seized weapons to Indian and Vietnamese armies, however no deal was reached after the withdrawal of the Chinese army from these two conflicts. The real cause for the conflict with India was the dispute in the border area, which both Chinese and India claimed, and the real cause for the conflict with Vietnam was the Vietnamese invasion into Cambodia because the Chinese government supported Khmer Rouge. As the disputes were not sealed through these two conflicts, it may suggest that (i) the operation led by the Chinese army was not aimed to settle the disputes; (ii) China did not have sufficient armed forces to settle the disputes; (iii) the withdrawal of the Chinese army might be due to other reasons, for example, worrying about the US involvement in the Sino-Indian war. This again is the way that China disengages from wars.

13.2 JAPANESE WAY TO DISENGAGE FROM WAR

When we look at the Japanese war history, we can clearly see a good possibility for Japan to disengage from the third Sino-Japanese war. Arguably Japan successfully disengaged from the first Sino-Japanese war, which means the war finished in favor of Japan without involvements of western powers. During the initial phase of the second Sino-Japanese war, the Japanese armed forces successfully occupied the northeast part of China, Manchuria, without engaging fully with the Chinese government.

The general pattern of Japanese disengagement from war seems as follows. The Japanese armed forces would launch a pre-emptive attack in order to be in a good position for further negotiation if the enemy is not strong enough. This is the clear case for the Japanese attack on the US during World War II when the Japanese armed forces hoped to destroy the US navy aircraft carriers in Pearl Harbor with their simultaneous invasions in several places along the Pacific Rim.

Although the Japanese armed forces could think of other approaches, a deadly pre-emptive attack on China, for example, Chinese army bases as well as other strategic targets, would be an important and good option for the Japanese armed forces. This is so because the Chinese tradition is not to launch a first attack, this tradition leads the Chinese people to hate a pre-emptive attack. For example, many Chinese people currently consider the Korean War very negatively because North Korea was first to launch the war. This tradition excludes the possibility that the Chinese armed forces would be the first one to attack Japan. On the other hand, Japanese history suggests the trend that the pre-emptive attack, or to be the first one to launch the attack is acceptable for the Japanese people. In fact, it seems to be the only way for Japanese armed forces to wage any war.

In such a case, it would be possible for Japan to attack China, and then rapidly disengage from the third Sino-Japanese war, even if both China and Japan declared war on each other. This is so because (i) the Japanese people are certainly the best nation familiar with Chinese history, culture and tradition through the common culture; (ii) the Japanese government is historically the best government familiar with the ways the Chinese government deals with foreign countries; (iii) the Japanese armed forces are most experienced in war with Chinese armed forces. Thus, they surely know the Chinese characteristics and behaviors very well, and can operate their attacks accordingly.

Chinese history suggests that the wars with China generally go along several phases: (i) the Chinese people and governments had no sense that a war is inevitable long before a war, (ii) the Chinese people, governments and armed forces were over-confident on their victory mainly due to some spirit power and their superiority before a war, (iii) the Chinese government was very likely to compromise the foreign demand after an initial disaster although at the very beginning the Chinese government and people appeared to be unconquerable and far superior over foreign invaders.

Still, history shows that the Chinese armed forces generally did not conduct the war into invaders' lands, if the Chinese armed forces defeated the invaders [5].

If all these Chinese war trends would still hold, then it would be very easy for Japan to disengage from the third Sino-Japanese war without losing anything. The Japanese armed forces would surely attack China first, then the Japanese government would make a good deal with the Chinese government and the Japanese people would remain happily in Japan.

In order to make a peace deal, it is highly probable that the Japanese air force would launch a pre-emptive attack on Chinese soil. On the other hand, the Chinese government would almost certain retreat from her position, and make a deal with Japan for the stability of China.

13.3 US' WAY TO DISENGAGE FROM WAR

Although the US has been attending endless wars and armed conflicts since the end of World War II, we have not observed a clear pattern on how the US would disengage from a war. This is so because in most cases we observed regarding the US were the undeclared wars, and the US are the absolutely stronger party in these undeclared wars and armed conflicts. These facts implicate that the US has a good possibility to disengage from these undeclared wars and armed conflicts.

In conjunction with World War II, the US' way to disengage from a war would be as follows. The best way for the US to disengage from a war would be to build a democratically elected government in the defeated country, and leave a certain amount of US troops stationed. The worst way for the US to disengage from a war is the Vietnam War.

On the military front, the US would find it relatively easy to disengage from a war if US ground troops would not be involved. The US seems to find it easy to disengage from a war in Europe and Africa, but difficult to disengage from a war in Asia.

The difficulty for the US to disengage from a war in Asia might be a factor in preventing the intervention from the US in the third Sino-Japanese war, which would pave the way for peace talks to solve disputes between China and Japan.

13.4 WHICH IS THE BEST?

Regarding disengagement from war, we should ask to what degree is disengagement possible?

If the strong party would completely destroy the weak party, then the disengagement would be considered well done. However, the remaining tasks would be huge. The strong party would need to build a new government, to work as police to maintain social order, to use taxpayers' money to rebuild the destroyed country, and so on and so forth. Moreover, the cost of life and money from the point that an earlier disengagement would be possible, to the point of completely destroying the weaker party, would be huge.

If we consider the disengagement as a process from a mutual will to disengage from a war to a unilateral will to disengage from a war, we might have more power to judge which way to disengage from a war would be the best.

Likely, a mutual will to disengage from a war would always be through various peace talks. This approach seems to be the solution for equal power conflicts and small-sized wars. Thus, the question raised here is whether there would be efficient and effective channels to conduct peace talks during the third Sino-Japanese war? This is possible because the third Sino-Japanese war would be an equal power conflict if the US, and NATO would not be involved. Can the UN mediate this peace talk? Can the UN build a buffer between China and Japan to promote a peace talk?

On the other hand, the peace talk would leave a completely hostile enemy country as we have seen in the disengagement in the Korean War and in Middle East.

At this stage, the US would play as big a role in disengagement from conflicts between China and Japan as the US' role in Middle East peace talk. Perhaps, it would be best to begin a peace talk now, even if the third Sino-Japanese war is far beneath the horizon, rather than to begin a peace talk when the real armed conflict occurs. This is so also because now the US still has much to say before her decay would be fully displayed.

Chapter 14

CHINA IN THE THIRD SINO-JAPANESE WAR

"We hope for the best," said he, "and pray that the gods may grant us the victory in this most momentous crisis. But we must remember that it is the greatest and the most momentous of human affairs that are always the most uncertain, and we can not foresee what is today to be the result of the battle. If it goes against us, what do you intend to do? Do you intend to escape, or to die?"
— Jacob Abbott, Cleopatra [25]

It is not very clear whether the politicians who launched a war considered what their country would be during the war, because it seems that most war planners who planned the war mainly concentrated their wisdom on the enemy country to consider how to destroy this enemy country as fast as possible.

If this would be the case for most wars in human history, it would be similar to a chess player who only looks at his opponent chessboard but pays no attention to his own side.

Perhaps, this strategy could be useful for the war without the air force and long-ranged missiles, for the country without any valuable infrastructure, and for the country having nothing to lose. Certainly, if one would launch a war on the US from Afghanistan, one should focus his efforts in finding the weakest point in the US rather than worry about the loss in Afghanistan from US retaliations. Therefore we might need to imagine the loss and suffering in China if the third Sino-Japanese war occurs because nowadays China and the Chinese people might have too many valuable things to lose.

14.1 WAR OUT OF MAINLAND CHINA

If the third Sino-Japanese war would occur out of Mainland China, this would be a big challenge for the Chinese government. At this stage, we could think of two potential problems.

The first would be the morale. Of course, this would not be a big problem at the beginning because the Chinese people are very patriotic. However, the soldiers and seamen suffering either in war on disputed islands or in sea blockades would be demoralized when they notice how leisure and luxurious lifestyles are conducted in Mainland China, and how rich people spend their money randomly for pleasure. This demoralization was once noted during the armed conflict between China and Vietnam in 1970s. China was still very poor but the comparison between soldiers on the front and the joyful life in small cities was dismaying.

On the other hand, we should admit that the reform in China has already changed the relationship between individual and government into a money-driven relationship, i.e. you pay me money I do your work. Under such circumstances, one might wonder whether China would use mercenaries? Of course, the demoralization would still be a small problem because China has a huge human resource.

However, the second problem would really be a big problem, which would be the stability of the government. Of course this is not a particular issue for the Chinese government, but for almost all governments around the world. This is so because history, including the Chinese history, shows that a government would be relatively easy to collapse if the war is conducted out of the territory in question. This further means that any government would be relatively unstable if the war conducted outside of their country results in failure or disaster. Actually, the government would fall if the war did not reach the expected consequence pictured in peoples minds.

By clear contrast, we would easily find that the government, no matter what type of government and no matter whether the government is popular, would quite firmly hold power in their hands with popular support when a foreign, armed force invades. In fact, many Chinese feudal dynasties and governments survived well in a corner of China, even when a large portion of China was occupied. No one claimed the government incompetent in most such cases.

Therefore, the Chinese government would face strong pressures from the Chinese people, from overseas Chinese people, and from the internal force inside the government itself if and when the third Sino-Japanese is conducted outside of Mainland China.

14.2 THE WAR SPREADING TO MAINLAND CHINA

If no foreign troops land in Mainland China, then China would still suffer heavily during air attacks as well as nuclear attacks. This is because the distance between Mainland China and Japan is too short to have any effective and efficient warnings. This means that the Chinese air force's aircrafts in the regions near Japan might still be largely grounded rather than able to take off into Chinese air space. Still it is not clear whether China has an early warning system to monitor the possible attack of intercontinental ballistic missile. Could the Chinese air force be able to defend the large Chinese air space from any attack? The likely answer, even the certain answer, would be No. In such a case, how could the local Beijing administration control the traffic in Beijing city during an air attack? This is the simplest question. How could people survive in Chinese mega cities when the traffic completely goes into chaos? This is another very simple question.

No matter whether the foreign force would land in Mainland China or not, gun control would be the biggest challenging problem for the Chinese government and Chinese society. This is because theoretically, the Chinese people have no right to possess any weapons and arm themselves. If we consider the size of the Chinese territory and the mobility of Chinese armed forces, we would not expect to see the case that the Chinese armed forces would arrive at landing places in time because China has so a large territory for airborne forces to land and has such a long seacoast for marine forces to land. Therefore, the Chinese armed forces would theoretically be unable to drive foreign armed forces immediately out of Chinese territory.

In such a case, would the Chinese government give the weapons to ordinary Chinese people to defend their country? Can we not ask whether these weapons would be used in different ways? Can we not assume that these distributed weapons would kill many local administrative staffs if we consider the current injustice and gap between rich and poor? Can we not assume that these distributed weapons would be used for looting? These distributed weapons would eventually endanger the stability of local authorities, because gangs could be organized, even local warlords would be formed.

If the local warlords would get foreign aid, then the situation in China would be totally different because we, the Chinese people, would once again face a civil war together with an invasion.

Chapter 15

CHINESE MILITARY STRATEGIC THOUGHTS

A civil war, indeed, is like the heat of a fever; but a foreign war is like the heat of exercise, and serveth to keep the body in health.
— Francis Bacon, Of the True Greatness of Kingdoms and Estates -- The Essays of Francis Bacon [1]

In Francis Bacon's sense, we could say that the traditional Chinese military strategy, military thoughts, and ancient military sages' thoughts are prescriptions to cure the heat of a fever, where oftentimes the remedy is worse than disease to our nation, rather than a remedy to make our nation healthier.

We could even consider that the traditional Chinese military strategy and thoughts are the side-product of constant Chinese disease, civil war and endless internal conflicts, therefore it is clear and evident that the Chinese military strategy and thoughts cannot be applied to the war with foreign countries no matter whether the war was conducted in Chinese soil or in foreign soil. Chinese history has already clearly demonstrated that China was defeated in almost all the wars with foreign invaders before the creation of the People's Republic of China although we, the Chinese people, have our ancient military sages' thoughts.

If we objectively look at the wars and conflicts after the creation of the People's Republic of China, our, the Chinese people's, mind would not be light.

We could say that we, the Chinese people, are losers in the Korean War, because the US troops have obtained the legal right to be permanently stationed in South Korea since the beginning of the Korean War although we, the Chinese people, have lost so many lives, but had withdrawn the Chinese troops from North Korea.

The Sino-Indian war did not solve any disputes between China and India, but China has to station a large amount of troops in these remote areas in Tibet. Moreover, this Sino-Indian war sowed seeds of hatred either in the Chinese or

Indian mind, more notably Indian minds, and China and India have become rivals in almost every aspect since then.

The conflict between China and the Soviet Union was also a bitter experience because China had to take a step back if not kneel down to the threat of nuclear attack from the Soviet Union.

The victory of the Vietnam War did not give China any advantage, besides worsening the relationship between China and Vietnam, and between China and Laos.

The most recent conflict with Vietnam did not guarantee the survival of the Khmer Rouge, which then the Chinese government weighed heavily on.

15.1 OFFENSIVE STRATEGY

In Chinese history, there was a general, Cheng Yaojin, who helped to create Dynasty Tang (618–907). This general, as legend told, was famous for striking his enemy three times with his great axe in any combat: if he could kill his enemy within these three strikes, then he would win; if he could not kill his enemy in these three strikes, then he would run away.

This is in fact a typical Chinese offensive strategy, for example, we can find that the Chinese armies made five significant phase offensives from October 1950 to April 1951 in the space of six months, then the Korean War went into a stalemate stage until the end of Korean war.

Similarly, we can see the similar military strategy during the second Sino-Japanese war: arguably the Kuomintang government's offensives practically finished in early 1940 after the Battle of Shanghai, Battle of Taierzhuang, Battle of Changsha, and other battles. Meanwhile, the Chinese Communist party's offensives practically finished after the Battle of Pingxingguan and Battle of Hundred of Regiments.

The Chinese military legend on General Cheng Yaojin and our review on the most modern wars, the second Sino-Japanese war and Korean War suggest that the traditional Chinese offensive strategy is shortsighted, because we, the Chinese military sages, expect to defeat strong enemies with a few strikes, after which we can only wait and consume ourselves in a painful no-action war.

A recent report in a Chinese newspaper specialized in military affairs had a title "Three fists smash the US aircraft carriers", which meant that the Chinese armies can use their missiles to destroy the US aircraft carriers. Let us take another example, a report in another Chinese newspaper specialized in military affairs wrote that the Chinese missiles could destroy the Taiwanese army within 20 or 30 minutes.

We should ask the editors and reporters on this type of reports: (i) do they consider the unconditional surrender of the US after three fists, (ii) do they consider the consequences and reactions from such an attack, (iii) do they consider the US aircraft carriers unmovable thus China can attack them without question, and so on and so forth?

Very likely, our Chinese military strategy and thoughts can only reach to this point, that is, China would launch a deadly attack, either pre-emptive or post-emptive, then wait for the surrender of our enemies.

Let us go further along this line: let us assume that the Chinese attack would be extremely successful, and our strong enemies would surrender immediately. Then what would the Chinese people and army do? Our Chinese military strategy and thoughts do not give us any clue or answer, so likely we would irresponsibly leave these countries into chaos, rather than to administer them. In such a case, would we, the Chinese people, organize an expeditionary force? The answer is almost certain. No, we, the Chinese people, would most likely stay within the Chinese border, and enjoy our narrow interests again, and not care about the "surrounded countries" anymore.

15.2 DEFENSIVE STRATEGY

Perhaps the famous and best defensive strategy against foreign invaders would be to destroy everything in order that the foreign invaders have no provision to advance. Military history has sufficiently shown the application of such a strategy.

However, there is almost no such case in Chinese military history, because the Chinese defensive strategy was developed from civil war, which could be read in the classical Chinese novel, Three Kingdoms and Romance of Three Kingdoms [26]:

> Adviser Zheng Du said, "Although Liu Bei has been successful and captured cities and towns, yet his army is but small, his hosts are not near him, and he depends upon chance for his grain and has no proper supplies. Therefore our best plan is to remove the people of Baxi and Zitong to the farther side of River Fu, burn all the granaries, fortify the city, and let starvation defeat him. Let us reject all challenges to battle, and in a hundred days his troops will go off of their own accord. Then we can do with him as we will."

"I like not the plan," said Liu Zhang. "Oppose invaders in order that tranquillity may prevail is a well-worn maxim, but till now I have never heard of disturbing the people in order to oppose the march of an enemy. Your words are not such as safety."

By this defensive strategy, the previous warlords could buy the hearts of people under their governance in various Chinese civil wars, but could not defend against foreign invaders. Therefore we can see how foreign invaders could get necessary support from the area they occupied throughout Chinese history. On the other hand, we can arguably see how the Chinese people lived peacefully and happily under foreign governance, and there were almost no universal rebellions or riots in areas occupied by foreign invaders. Of course, the final consequence in occupied Chinese land is the so-called Chineselization [5], i.e. the foreign invaders had to use the Chinese officials to deal with all the administrative issues due to the complex Chinese language, then the foreign invaders would begin to enjoy a luxurious life as all the Chinese people enjoy and lose their valor for fighting and conquering. Finally the foreign invaders' dynasties or governments would be overthrown by the Chinese people and would go home. The Chineselization would arguably be the traditional Chinese defensive strategy against foreign invaders although this process might take several hundred years as Chinese history shows.

However, if China would adopt a new defensive strategy by evacuating Chinese people and destroying everything in the evacuated areas, then it would mean that China is preparing for foreign invaders to land in Chinese soil. The next question would be where the foreign invaders would come from? Nevertheless, South Korea and North Korea would be the most important buffer zone to prevent the Japanese armies and the US troops from invading, however can we not expect to see the Indian troops across the Himalayan Mountains to reach Tibet? Do we consider the evacuation of Tibet? Do we really dare destroy our valuable global mega cities along the Chinese seacoast?

15.3 PRE-EMPTIVE

As the Chinese military strategy and thoughts were mainly developed in pre-industrialization time, the pre-emptive attack did not appear to be an important military strategy, because it did really not matter much whether a party took the pre-emptive strategy with armies equipped with cold weapons.

Since the creation of the People's Republic of China, the pre-emptive strategy was labeled as invaders' strategy, while China seems to adopt the so-called post-emptive, hou fa zhi ren, in Chinese pronunciation. Therefore, China should prepare to stand the first, second, even several waves of attacks before launching Chinese post-emptive attacks. The serious question raised here is whether the Chinese government, Chinese armies and Chinese people can withstand these massive pre-emptive attacks?

On the other hand, if China formally abandons her so-called post-emptive strategy, then the immediate question is whether China really plans a pre-emptive attack on Japan, or on the US, or on other NATO countries, because the pre-emptive attack on any one of these countries is the same as provoking the application of security treaties among these countries. Still, if China formally abandons her so-called post-emptive strategy, but has no intention of launching a pre-emptive attack, then this abandonment would certainly provide a pretext to provoke pre-emptive attacks on Chinese soil.

15.4 SURVEILLANCE

During the second Sino-Japanese war, it seems that the Chinese government as well as local warlords did not have any information on the possibility of occurrence of the Mukden Incident and the Marco Polo Bridge Incident as well as following battles in different areas inside China. Otherwise the Chinese government as well as local warlords would have done some preparations for these incidents and battles. Therefore we should ask whether the Chinese governments or warlords had any workable intelligence service? No doubt, the Chinese governments and warlords had their Chinese version of intelligence service, however these agents seemed not to be able to get any useful and reliable information, or penetrate into the Japanese policymaking center.

If we extend our view into Chinese history, we would see that previous Chinese dynasties did not have any reliable information on the possibilities that severely military conflicts would take place between Chinese empires and foreign invaders. Generally, China and her governments/dynasties were not prepared for any invasion or armed conflicts.

If we take our view to the contemporary Chinese history, we would feel that the Chinese Communist Red Army did not have any confirmed information on five offences made by Kuomintang armies. Therefore the Chinese Communist Red Army simply waited for the attacks, which could be launched at any time, without any counter-attacks.

These facts simply suggest that the surveillance system does not occupy any significant position in Chinese military strategy and thoughts. If we look at the so-called Thirty-Six Stratagems [21] developed by ancient Chinese military sages, we could hardly find any stratagem on how to monitor and spy on the enemies, but most stratagems concentrate how to play a tricky game in order to make the third party lose, and then obtain some benefits. The shortage of surveillance systems is again the product of Chinese long-term civil wars, which can be used in low-speed civil wars. Actually, we could reasonably guess that the civil wars in Chinese history, for the most part, were quite slow compared to modern war.

The above discussion is mainly focused on the wars conducted inside Chinese territory. If we would extend our view a little bit longer, we could say that China did not have any reliable information on the possible Vietnamese invasion into Cambodia. Similarly, our surveillance system also did not predict the possible armed conflict between China and the Soviet Union in 1960s..

This raises a serious question on whether the Chinese surveillance systems or intelligence services or simply spies can find any Japanese pre-emptive attacks on the Chinese armies and territory? Without such a surveillance system, how can China conduct counter-attacks?

If the Chinese surveillance system could not provide any reliable information, how could we expect it to provide any reliable information on remote countries such as the US and NATO countries?

15.5 KNOWLEDGE ON MODERN WAR

As civil wars prevailed in China for thousands of years, the Chinese armies had fewer chances to across Chinese borders to meet any foreign troops, therefore the Chinese army traditionally is lacking in knowledge of modern war, as we read [17]:

"For the next few days nothing was talked of but the war, and many Chinese generals were received in audience by Her Majesty. These audiences were sometimes very amusing, as these soldiers were quite unaccustomed to the rules of the Court and did not know the mode of procedure when in the presence of Her Majesty. Many foolish suggestions were made by these generals. During one of the conversations Her Majesty remarked on the inefficiency of the navy and referred to the fact that we had no trained naval officers. One of the generals replied that we had more men in China than in any other country, and as for ships, why we had dozens of river boats and China merchant boats, which could be used in case of war. Her Majesty ordered him to retire, saying that it was perfectly true that we had plenty of men in China, but that the majority of them were like himself, of very little use to the country. After he had retired, everybody commenced to laugh, but Her Majesty stopped us, saying that she did not feel at all like laughing, she was too angry to think that such men held positions as officers in the army and navy. One of the Court ladies asked me why Her Majesty was so angry with the man for mentioning the river boats, and was very much surprised when I informed her that the whole of them would be worse than useless against a single war vessel."

The long-term peace in China in fact makes the Chinese people short of knowledge on modern war, thus we have the Chinese proverbs, such as to fight only on paper, Zhi Shang Tan Bing, in Chinese pronunciation. An recent example seems to be that a Chinese major general said that China could bomb Japan and her allies back two hundreds years. This statement can be viewed as a shortage in modern war, and as our Chinese proverb says: Ma Su's words exceed his deeds, And he does not make much use, Ma Su Yan Guo Qi Shi, Zhong Wu Da Yong, in Chinese pronunciation [27].

15.6 DOUBLE GAMES

The Chinese people are very proud of our ancient Chinese military sages, who could skillfully play a double game to alter the war direction. In Chinese military history, mainly in legendary classical novels, we can see how these super clever military sages used their talent to persuade kings or warlords to attack other kingdoms or regions or stop planned wars.

If we look at the so-called Thirty-Six Stratagems [21] again, we could find that most of stratagems are related to playing double games.

So can the modern Chinese people follow our ancestors to play a double game, which was advocated by ancient Chinese military sages, to prevent the predictable involvement of Japanese's allies? Or does China have any options to prevent the intervention from Japanese's allies?

Perhaps the double game would be efficient for a civil war occurring inside China, during which mostly a stronger party (kingdom or warlord) would like to play a double game with small parties (kingdoms or warlords). On an international stage, we could arguably say that various parties played the double game before World War II, for example, we could arguably consider the Munich Agreement and Molotov-Ribbentrop Pact as results of double games.

However, it seems what a double game obtains was the time, precious time before the war. If this is the case, we should expect to see the Chinese strategists to play double games now because it seems that the third Sino-Japanese war would be inevitable.

However, an important fact, which prevents the advocates of traditional Chinese military strategy and thoughts from playing a double game, is that any double game at an international level needs to sign a mutual treaty between two countries, while China has no intention of being involved in any international treaties. This is so because the so-called double game in Chinese military strategy and thoughts is to use sweet words to persuade a third party to bear the loss that the player should suffer. This is a very selfish and simple game, which unfortunately can no longer be played in this time.

Chapter 16

MOST UNIMAGINABLE SCENARIOS

Imagination is more important than knowledge . . .
— Albert Einstein

Before ending this book, let us imagine several completely unimaginable scenarios related to the third Sino-Japanese war under very particular circumstances.

For any unimaginable scenarios, the most important issue is that we need to know through which approach these unimaginable scenarios could come to true, i.e. we should have a clear roadmap to reach these unimaginable scenarios.

Historically, the politicians and military planners seemed not to like to imagine the unimaginable scenarios, but seemed to like to imagine the war in favoring politicians and military planners' predictions. Actually, we could arguably say that the consequence of World War II was unimaginable for the politicians and military planers before the launching of World War II.

16.1 NEW QUEEN IN MEDITERRANEAN SEA

If the third Sino-Japanese war would occur in full scale, then NATO's involvement would be fully expected. Then, we will see the vacuum in the Mediterranean Sea. Can Turkey and Iran together dominate the Mediterranean Sea while world powers concentrate on East Asia?

This could be possible, though unimaginable, because it is suggested that Islamism would prevail in the world in the 21st century. Actually we have already witnessed the strong rise of Islamism worldwide since the beginning of the 21st century.

Now the question is whether it would be difficult for Turkey to dominate Mediterranean Sea? At the current time, it is very unlikely, not only because Turkey is a member of NATO, but also the US sixth fleet controls the Mediterranean Sea. So the precondition seems to be Turkey's departure from NATO, which is also unimaginable,

Actually Turkey and Iran both have full potential to become a world power. This is so because both Turkey and Iran meet the first request to become a world power, i.e. the size of population is larger than 50,000,000 [5]. What they then need is [5] (i) a systematical idea or theory related to social justice and fair distribution of social wealth to shine over the ideological concepts of the US, (ii) some type of entitlement, actually, Iran already has her regional entitlement in the Middle East, we would have no difficulty in imagining that Iran would expend her regional entitlement to other places, and (iii) the opportunity, which would be provided by the third Sino-Japanese war followed by World War III.

16.2 DESTROYING ISRAEL

If a full-scale third Sino-Japanese war would occur, then World War III should follow. However World War III would be very different from World War I and II, where European powers were mainly players and Europe was the main battlefield. Therefore, the Middle East would become a place that no western powers would pay too much attention to during World War III. This would provide a really great opportunity for Arabian people to drive Israeli out of Middle East.

This could be possible, though unimaginable, because the US would not have a free hand to deal with the issue in Middle East. We should consider that the third Sino-Japanese war would not occur tomorrow but some time in the future. This future suggests that it would be possible that several Arabian nations would have nuclear weapons, thus the Israeli nuclear retaliation would not be as dreadful as Arabian nations view now.

Actually, the recently armed conflict between Israel and Hezbollah indicates that Hezbollah's threat to attack popular Israeli cities could arguably prevent Israel from bombing the center of Beirut.

If several Arabian countries would have nuclear weapons in hand, then the third Sino-Japanese war, World War III, would project a situation similar to the time before World War II, when the Middle East was in Arabian hands since the last crusader expedition.

16.3 ENDING OF AMERICAN CENTURY BY UNITED FORCES

Another unimaginable scenario could be that China, Korea, Japan and Russia would unite to end the American century. Of course, this would be totally unimaginable. However, history is ironically unpredictable therefore we could not exclude any unimaginable scenarios from our analysis and consideration.

In fact, it would be more correct to say that it would not be the united forces from China, Korea, Japan and Russia that would end the American century, but the US herself. Let us face the serious facts. The ideologies advocated by the US have lost their momentum day by day, because the so-called free market economy can now be seen anywhere in the world. The democratic elections can also be seen in many countries in the world while the US uses her taxpayers' money to support some dictatorships in the world. Still, the US is no longer the world power house. Can we not assume that the US would be in default within next 50 to 100 years with her current borrowing speed?

If an ideology would once again prevail around the world, can we not exclude the possibility that Japan would follow as she cannot find any other way to get out her decade-long recession? If Japan would change the course with another ideology, the western Pacific Ocean would not partially belong to the US.

16.4 SPRING AND AUTUMN/WARRING STATES PERIOD

The Spring and Autumn period (770 BC to 476 BC) and Warring States period (475 BC to 221 BC) are two particular periods in ancient Chinese history, during which the war frequently occurred between different states without constant alliance.

Can we not imagine that the world, during the third Sino-Japanese war as well as the following World War III, would fall into such state, i.e. there would be no constant alliance? This could be possible because the current dominated power, the US, would be much weaker in the future than now with respect to her contribution to the world economy. Under such circumstances, several countries would have somewhat equal economic power with somewhat equal military power, for example, Brazil, China, India, Japan, Russia, and the US, we could not even exclude the possibility of the emergence of Iran and a united Korea with somewhat equal military power and less equal economic power.

If these would be the cases, then it would not be important whether a country would form an alliance with the US to secure her safety, especially if the US would suffer too much in terms of her economic and military power during the third Sino-Japanese war as well as World War III.

Then the world would like the current pharmaceutical market, where no single pharmaceutical company could dominate the whole market as Microsoft does in the computer operating system market.

Still, if no ideology would prevail around the world, then capitalism would perhaps lose her shining points due to the constant increase of jobless people and all the economic power following the capitalism mechanism. If so, it would be hard to form any ideological bloc in the world as a military alliance. Under such an assumption, we might expect to see the "the Spring and Autumn period and Warring States period".

Another possible case should be referred to China, if many warlords would appear in China either due to gun control problem (Section 14.2, Chapter 14) or due to foreign supports, these warlords would once again lead China into bloody civil war. Arguably, the endless Chinese civil before the second Sino-Japanese war was largely the consequence of the first Sino-Japanese war, i.e. the defeated Chinese feudal dynasty fell, and many new warlords supported by different foreign powers began to expend their influence and controlled area. Actually, we could recall the case in Afghanistan, where Afghanistan fell into long-term civil war after the withdrawal of Soviet troops.

16.5 ENDING OF CIVILIZATION

If the third Sino-Japanese war as well as the following World War III would go against politicians and military planners' predictions, then these politicians and military planners would lose their mind, and desperately try to turn the course of the war. In such a case, they might crazily use the nuclear weapons without considering the consequences.

If this were the case, then Africa and Latin America would not be free from nuclear pollution with the complete destruction of Asian, American and European cities.

The forgotten nuclear winter would come, then arguably it would be the end of civilization.

Chapter 17

FINAL REMARK

I know not with what weapons World War III will be fought, but World War IV will be fought with sticks and stones.
— Albert Einstein

Historically, Japan is a country that sometimes made wrong decisions. For example, Japan could colonize China if Japan did not join the Axis during World War II or at least the second Sino-Japanese war would have been extended. Similarly, China is also a country that frequently made wrong decisions. Therefore, the question of the third Sino-Japanese war would rely on whether China or Japan would make a wrong decision.

Until now, China seems to have done everything that it deems necessary to become a world power, for example, fast economic growth, Olympic games, and so on and so forth. However, China is still not a world power, nor a political center. This issue would torture the Chinese people who dream a super powerful China. However, we still cannot fully answer the following questions after exhausted options: (i) Can China become a Pacific empire without war with Japan or war with the US? (ii) Can China become a world power without war? (iii) Can China settle and seal her disputes with other countries forever without war? We hope for positive answers to the above questions, because the third Sino-Japanese could be avoidable, otherwise the possible prevention of the third Sino-Japanese war would be doom.

China and Japan have already had two wars. Both the Chinese people and Japanese people suffered a lot. For the sake of both the Chinese people and Japanese people, for the sake of possible suffering of world people during the third Sino-Japanese war, possibly followed by World War III, we should do our best to maintain the peace in both China and Japan.

For some politicians, the engagement of war looks more like a political game, through which those politicians could hopefully gain their popularity in order to get more votes in the next election or to enforce their existing power either in their party or in their administration. The politicians have fooled both the Chinese people and the Japanese people with their personal ambitions, which resulted in the first and second Sino-Japanese wars.

Historically, the positions of China and Japan are somewhat similar to France and England. When both England and France fought each other for years, neither China nor Japan had the capacity to cross the open sea between China and Japan. When both England and France realized that they both have common interests, China and Japan became rivals and wanted to defeat each other.

Can we not say that we, the Chinese people and Japanese people, lag a hundred of years behind compared with the British and French people in this regard? This is because what we are doing was done many years ago in reference to the relationship between England and France.

For the sake of the people in both China and Japan, we, the Chinese people and Japanese people, should live peacefully as the French people and British people do.

On the other hand, the analyses in this book suggest that the third Sino-Japanese war would mean that China would use her single country force against the whole civilized world. This is an unprecedented case in human history simply because no single country can defeat all the countries in the world, no single country can win such a war.

In the past, France tried to use her single country power to fight against all the European powers, but failed. Germany tried to use her single country power to fight against the world, but failed. Similarly, the Soviet Union tried to use her and her satellites' power with Marxism and Leninism to conquer the world but failed too.

Anyone who hopes to see a strong and prosperous China would not hope to see the third Sino-Japanese war because the joint forces from Japan, US, and NATO will certainly defeat China. This is so because human history until now did not show any case that a single country could defeat the rest of world, even China now is still not the number one world power.

Therefore, if we, the Chinese people, launch the third Sino-Japanese war, we would risk the Chinese as a nation. On the other hand, if Japan would launch the third Sino-Japanese war followed by World War III, we would risk the world civilization.

Hence, we, the people loving world peace, should do our best to prevent politicians from going along a dangerous road to the end of civilization.

REFERENCES

[1]   Bacon, F. (1625) *Of Boldness - The Essays of Francis Bacon*. A free ebook from http://manybooks.net/.

[2]   King-Hall, S. (1918) *Diary of a U-boat Commander*. A free ebook from http://manybooks.net/.

[3]   Maruyama, S. (1969) *Battle of the Japan Sea*. Film.

[4]   Cumings, B. (2010) *Dominion from Sea to Sea: Pacific Ascendancy and American Power*. Yale University Press.

[5]   Wu, G. (2009). *China: Has the Last Opportunity Passed by?!* New York: Nova Science Publishers.

[6]   Abbott,   J   (1857).   *Richard   I.   The   Baldwin   Project.* http://www.mainlesson.com/display.php?author=abbottandbook=richard1an dstory=_contents.

[7]   Adams, B. (1913). *The theory of social revolutions*. Project Gutenberg EBook #10613 http://www.gutenberg.org/files/10613 /10613-h/ 10613-h.htm.

[8]   Miki Hayden, G. (1998) *Pacific Empire*. JONA Books, 1 edition.

[9]   Sun, T. *Translated by Giles, L. The Art of War.* A free ebook from http://manybooks.net/.

[10]   Wu, G. (2010). *USA-United States of Asia: An Asian Union Initiative*. New York: Nova Science Publishers.

[11]   Mao, Z.D. (1930). *A single spark can start a prairie fire.* http://www.marxists.org/reference/archive/mao/selected-works/volume-1/mswv1_6.htm.

[12]   Wu, G. (2011). *China 1966-1976: Cultural Revolution Revisited - Can It Happen Again?* New York: Nova Science Publishers.

[13]   Defoe,   D.   (1719).   *Robinson   Crusoe.*   A   free   ebook   from http://manybooks.net/.

[14] Dumas, A. (1998). *The Count of Monte Cristo*. Project Gutenberg Ebook #1184.

[15] Thucydides. *The History of the Peloponnesian War*. Project Gutenberg Ebook #7142 http://www.gutenberg.org/cache/ epub/ 7142/pg7142.txt

[16] *http://en.wikipedia.org/wiki/Chinese_spirit_possession.*

[17] Ling, D. (1911). *Two Years in the Forbidden City*. A free ebook from http://manybooks.net/.

[18] Roosevelt, T. (1913). *An Autobiography*. A free ebook from http://manybooks.net/.

[19] *http://thinkexist.com/quotation/nations-have-no-permanent-friends-or-allies-they/771609.html.*

[20] *http://en.wikipedia.org/wiki/Bermeja.*

[21] *http://en.wikipedia.org/wiki/Thirty-Six_Stratagems.*

[22] *http://en.wikipedia.org/wiki/Warring_States_Period.*

[23] Abbott, J. (1849). *Hannibal*. The Baldwin Project. http://www. mainlesson.com/display.php?author=abbottandbook=hannibalandstory=_co ntents.

[24] http://threekingdoms.com/087.htm to http://threekingdoms.com/090.htm.

[25] Abbott, J. (1851). *Cleopatra*. A free ebook from http://manybooks.net/.

[26] *http://threekingdoms.com/064.htm.*

[27] *http://threekingdoms.com/085.htm.*

INDEX